THE MOST INCREDIBLE OLYMPIC STORIES

THE MOST INCREDIBLE OLYMPIC STORIES

LUCIANO WERNICKE

PAPER MISSILE
NIYOGI BOOKS

Published by
NIYOGI BOOKS
Block D, Building No. 77,
Okhla Industrial Area, Phase-I,
New Delhi-110 020, INDIA
Tel: 91-11-26816301, 26818960
Email: niyogibooks@gmail.com
Website: www.niyogibooksindia.com

Original title: Historias insólitas de los Juegos Olimpicos

Editor: Arkaprabha Biswas
Design: Shashi Bhushan Prasad

ISBN: 978-93-91125-14-1
Publication: 2021

Printed at: Niyogi Offset Pvt. Ltd., New Delhi, India

To my children, Facu and Nico

'And although the oblivion, which destroys everything, has killed my old illusion, I keep hidden a humble hope that is the whole fortune of my heart.'

—Alfredo Le Pera, *Volver*

CONTENTS

INTRODUCTION

An Olympic game is the sporting event par excellence. Although in many countries football is the discipline of choice and its World Cup is the summit of passion, it is also true that the Games arouse enormous fervour for its quantity and variety of competitions, because women take part and because in the two-week duration of the tournament, all countries participate and not only thirty-two, as is currently the case with the top FIFA event.

Oxford Dictionary indicates that an Olympiad is 'a major international contest in a particular game, sport, or scientific subject,' despite its original definition indicates something else: 'a period of four years between Olympic Games, used by the ancient Greeks in dating events'.

It is true, but as a counterpart it can be specified that in that same menu there are 33 competitions divided into 339 events, including football, basketball, tennis, volleyball, athletics and swimming, to name only the popular ones. However, each one has its own World Cup, yet for most, the zenith is the Olympic gold medal. In any case, it is not necessary to choose between the Olympic Games or the FIFA Cup: the two competitions coexist perfectly in the world sports calendar, both in every four years and interspersed 'two by two' so that everyone can enjoy an event considered as the 'modern war' for being a healthy, positive fight, and as a song affirms, 'the only fair of battles'.

In ancient Greece, the Games were sacred and all types of war action were banned throughout the week of the competitions. Upon resurgence in 1896 and reaching a formidable popularity throughout the planet in the 20th century, the Olympics became the scene of contests that extended beyond the boundaries of a court or stadium. Political propaganda actions, serious diplomatic friction and even a massacre—product of an ancient conflict—contaminated the purity of the sport, which was stopped only by the effect of the two world wars. Between 1948 and 1992, the United States and the former Union of Soviet Socialist Republics (USSR) discovered that the Games represented a perfect terrain to extend the 'Cold War' that, in parallel, was raging on other fronts.

In Munich 1972, the Olympiad developed 'normally', until in the middle of the competition, a Palestinian terrorist group executed eleven Israeli athletes. In that same country, but thirty-six years earlier, the Games allowed Adolf Hitler to extend his effective 'propaganda' beyond its borders. In Mexico 1968, a group of African-American athletes denounced the social abuse suffered by the black population in the United States.

It is important to clarify that this work reviews only the editions of the Summer Games, considering that the Winter Olympics are not 'universal' for two circumstances: one, because to do winter sports you need 'yes or yes' snow or ice, and this climatical phenomenon only happens naturally in the half (or less than the half) of the countries, only for a few months a year and in localities with certain geographical characteristics, usually mountain. In most of South America, Africa, the Caribbean, Central America, Southeast Asia and Oceania the snowfall is extraordinary or nil, so it is impossible for their populations to have universal access to this kind of recreations in which the people have to slide and not to run or jump. There have been cases of participants from tropical countries in the Winter Games, but these were atypical situations, closer to curiosity than to high competition. In Pieonchang 2018, the latest edition, ninety-two countries participated, a record for this version. In the last three Summer Games, more than 200 states competed. Rio de Janeiro 2016 reached all the nations of the globe affiliated to the IOC: 206.

Secondly, the practice of these winter disciplines necessarily requires the use of high-cost equipment, consisting of thermal suits, gloves, glasses and skis, as well as boards, skates and sleds. Later in this book we will see that the runner Abebe Bikila, from poor Ethiopia, won the 1960 Rome marathon dressed just in a shirt, shorts and bare feet. In ancient times, athletes used to compete naked, which matched the chances of each contestant. Currently, the possibilities of a good bobsleigh team necessarily depend on the quality of its very expensive sled.

Another key point in the Olympic history is 'amateurism'. Since the resurrection of the Games in 1896, the French baron Pierre de Coubertin imposed the exclusive participation of athletes who did not act in any sport as professionals, including non-Olympic disciplines. The American James Thorpe, an aboriginal 'all terrain' sportsman model, won by a very wide margin the pentathlon and decathlon of the Stockholm 1912 edition, but he was later disqualified when it was revealed that he had played baseball for money in a league in his country. The brilliant athlete, who also stood out in American football, claimed until the last of his days the return of his gold medals.

Coubertin's unfair stance—which the International Olympic Committee held firmly until the 1980s and finally abolished in 1992—was classist and contradictory. Classist, because it reserved the Olympic glory for children of wealthy families who could prepare for high competition without taking up their time working to maintain and afford trips and stays to the Games. Many participants had professions not related to sports and have won medals, but they were almost exceptions. The fact that some athletes had to occupy most of the day in trades, far from physical development, to obtain their livelihood, and others could train at pleasure every day because they were born with the golden spoon, implies that the concept of 'Amateurism' was synonymous to monstrous inequalities. The olive tree of the first Games was reserved almost exclusively for nobles and millionaires. At the 1968 Grenoble Winter Games, the president of the IOC, the American Avery Brundage, refused to hand over the medals to the Frenchman Jean-Claude Killy (winner of three golds in slalom, giant slalom and descent) and to the Canadian Nancy Greene (gold in giant slalom), because both had posed for graphic reporters with their skis in hand to display the brand of products. But he did award Peggy Fleming, gold in figure skating. Fleming didn't need sponsors: his father, a billionaire, had built an ice rink for his exclusive use in his own home.

Amateurism was jointly unworthy because it allowed undercover professionalism. During the second half of the 20th century, athletes from the former Soviet Union and its satellite countries (East Germany, Czechoslovakia, Romania, Hungary, Poland, etc.) were mostly registered in the official forms of the Games as policemen or army personnel of their country. However, this was a gross masquerade, since they were completely dedicated to training and rarely accomplished the tasks they claimed to perform. It was never clear why State support was allowed but not the private one.

Conscious of the prolific and diverse European and North American bibliography, the statistics recorded on the official website of the IOC and the infinite world of the Internet, I preferred to address the chronicle from another angle. Without abandoning the remarkable sporting feats, heroes and outstanding records, *The Most Incredible Olympic Stories* emphasises the most surprising curiosities and anecdotes that, at the same time, amuse and present a more human profile of the protagonists. Many of the stories are based on situations generated by politics, economics or complex sports regulations. Others, of countless eventualities. Like any other person, elite athletes, modern 'gods of the Olympus', suffer injuries and illnesses, robberies, theft, get drunk, hit rivals or referees, fall in love, get married or divorced, have children, fall asleep or lose some essential component of their competition equipment. Some succumb to the power of money, others prefer not to sell their honour.

They also live adventures that seem designed by Hollywood scriptwriters: a target-shooting champion who lost his right hand in the war and educated his left one to win the gold medal; an exhausted marathoner who had to run quickly in the opposite direction for more than a kilometer chased by a fierce dog; a Portuguese runner who was hit by a car, and ten days later won the Los Angeles marathon, with a record included; a sailor who left his career to rescue two drowning rivals; an athlete with two penises; a shooter ejected from the Olympic team for his noisy farts and a twin who replaced her sister star. These are just some of the more than 400 stories that feed this powerful cocktail of Olympic adventures.

Luciano Wernicke

Buenos Aires, September 2020

ANTIQUITY AND RENAISSANCE

A race of only 192.28 meters in length. That humble, that simple, that brief was the beginning of the Olympic Games. A modest test with a humble winner: a chef from the Elis region called Coroebo (or Koroibos or Choroebus, according to different translations). In the year 776 BC, he ran faster than any other competitor the distance of 'one stadium' and returned to his city crowned with olive twigs. Was the chef the first champion of the first Olympiad? Many historians asseverated that Coroebo was not the inaugural winner, but his name was the first to be engraved in stone at the head of a long series of heroes, also mentioned in poems of Homer or Pindar.

The foot race was part of a variety of religious and cultural rites that took place every four years, over six days, in a plain located next to the sanctuary of the city of Olympia, famous for its temple dedicated to Zeus, one of the seven wonders of the antiquity. It is estimated that the pedestrian test would have begun to be disputed at least 150 years before Coroebo, although this is only a conjecture.

Beyond its origin, after the victory of the chef, the games were consolidated and, through their successive editions, they grew in number of participants, who came first from all corners of the Hellenic world and later, from the different provinces of the Roman Empire. Likewise, other tests were added to the simple 192.28-meter contest:

a two-stadium race (called diaulium, 385 meters), four stadiums (769 meters), eight stadiums (1.538 meters) and up to twenty-four stadiums (known as Doric, 4.614 meters). Then, the pentathlon appeared (a competition that combined five disciplines: race, discus throwing, javelin throwing, long jump and fight), hoplitodromia (race wearing armor and carrying spear and shield), pugilism and horse-quadrigas. Boxing began with no difference of categories by weight or protection of any kind. The duels had no assault limit and ended by knockout or abandonment of one of the fighters. Over the years, leather strips were incorporated to protect the hands and make the blows stronger. Some boxers added small stones, lead fragments or wood chips to the straps to cause more damage to their rivals. The fights generated so much passion among the public that a new type of contest was added, designed especially for those who enjoyed the blood: the pancracy, an 'everything's fair' kind of *carnival*, that included bites, asphyxiation, kicks in the testicles and even sinking the fingers in the eyes of the rival. This new addition extended the Olympic calendar to seven days.

Since its inception, the games were conceived as a period of spiritual and religious recollection. Shortly after, they were dressed with a nationalist halo. In the 9th century BC, the kings Ifitos of Élide, Cleóstenes of Pisa and Licurgo of Esparta instituted what is known as the 'Olympic truce', an initiative that suspended all kinds of war actions between the Greek city states during the week of the games. They also established a ban on entering Olimpia, 'a sacred place', armed,—'Who dares to penetrate it with weapons will be considered sacrilegious'.

But not everyone could particpate in the competition. In the early days, only the Greek males were considered as 'free men'—legitimate sons with full possession of all civil rights, who had not committed anything sacrilegous ever. Then, for political reasons, contestants from other nations were accepted, in some cases by imposition, as happened with the Roman emperor Nero. The rules and codes of competence were engraved on bronze tables located in one of the temples of Olympia. The contestants had to arrive in the city at least four weeks before the beginning of the competition, to establish themselves in a kind of 'campground' where training was alternated with the study of competition rules, and where everyone had to take an oath that guarranted respect for the decisions of the judges and 'loyalty for the competition'. In the 5th century BC, during the final of the boxing tournament, a participant named Cleómedes killed his opponent. The judges disqualified him because they suspected in him some sort of a malice and a sense of trechery to the spirit of the game, and named champion 'post mortem' to his rival.

The winners only received a crown made with leaves and twigs of olive as a prize. However, their exploits gained importance to such an extent among their countrymen from the different city states, that they enjoyed benefits not far from that of the current government celebrities—tax exemptions, life pensions, houses, food and other goods allowed the heroes to enjoy a life relaxed and luxurious.

What was the role of women in the Games? Priamarily, there were no competitions reserved for them in the Olympic calendar. They only performed in some kind of a manifestation that juxtaposed sport and art in honour of the goddess Hera, which was held at another time of the year. Only single women and girls were allowed to attend Olympia as spectators. Married women were prohibited from witnessing the different sports, under the penalty of death. The only known case of violation of these rules corresponded to Callipatria, a woman who disguised herself as a man to see her son Pisidoro in the boxing competition. When the young man prevailed in the last fight, Callipatria forgot about the harsh rules, and overwhelmed by emotion, pounced on Pisidoro to hug him, not noticing that the linen cloth covering her face and hair dropped. The judges and spectators discovered the deception, but the woman was forgiven for being a daughter, sister and mother of Olympic champions.

The Olympics of antiquity ran until 394 BC, when they were abolished by the Roman emperor Theodosius I at the request of the Milan bishop, Aurelius Ambrosius (later St. Ambrosius), who considered them immoral and promoters of atheism. The decree not only prohibited the Games but also established the death penalty for those who tried to reissue them. Half a century later, another monarch, Theodosius II, ordered the destruction of all the temples of Olympia. To this brutal Roman disposition was added a series of earthquakes that ended up burying the remains, which remained hidden for twelve centuries. In the mid-19th century, a group of European archaeologists discovered the old ruins and the light illuminated the Olympic glory again. A few decades later, a French nobleman, Pierre de Frédy, Baron de Coubertin, came up with the crazy idea of returning life and greatness to the majestic Olympic Games. Well, not so crazy. The Theodosians were no longer there to enforce their absurd orders.

NERO, THE CHAMPION

Many monarchs and emperors of ancient times decided to participate in the Games to demonstrate their aptitudes in sport. Philip II, king of Macedonia and father of Alexander the Great, won horse and chariot races in 356 BC. Another contestant was the Roman Nero. The history books and the movie *Quo Vadis* expose the emperor as a vain and murderous psychopath. In spite of ordering bloodthirsty campaigns, liquidating his rivals and even his mother, a brother and his first two wives (the second, Popea, was killed by Nero by a savage kick in the stomach that caused an abortion and death due to bleeding), the despot supported the development of the arts and ordered the construction of numerous theaters and schools. Nero believed himself a descendant of Apollo and owner of an unmatched talent for music and poetry. However, the only ones who applauded and cheered their works, and interpretations were the members of a ridiculous claque that earned generous salaries to flatter the monarch's ears. In 67 BC, the emperor became obsessed with the Olympic Games and set out to win an olive crown. At any cost. The tyrant enrolled in the chariot race and bribed his rivals so that, as the competition spread, they were dropping out. Nero finished the race by running alone, and won despite having fallen awkwardly in a curve. The Greeks looked to the sky to question their gods. Little would have cost them to break the dictator's neck.

NUDITY

Anthropologists give different genealogies to the ancient tradition competing naked in the Olympics. In fact, several researchers show off this tradition—they point out that it would have been impossible for equestrian sports, for example—although most of the vessels with Olympic motifs represent athletes without any clothes. Some claim that, with nudity, women were forbidden to participate. Others claim that it provided a situation of social equality for the participants. Although at first all must be Greeks and free men, competition without clothes uniformed nobles with commoners, rich with poor. Another version—presumably closer to the fable than to reality—argues that Orsippus, a runner from Megara, an ancient Greek city in the prefecture of Attica, gained fame in his time for running naked in the 15th edition of stadium race, in the year 720 BC. According to the story, the sprinter got rid of the 'loincloth' or kind of shorts he used, in the middle of the test and, in a quick maneuver, he took it off and continued 'as God brought him into the world'. His victory, some historians said, marked an example to follow that soon became a tradition.

OLD STARS

Leonidas of Rhodes was probably the greatest athlete of antiquity. The records found by archaeologists give him twelve victories in four consecutive editions of the Games, both in speed and long-distance races. He prevailed in the events of the stadium, diaulos and dolics between the years 164 and 152 BC.

The wrestler Milon of Crotone (city located in the heel of the italic boot) won the title in 540 BC and he defended it successfully four times in a row until losing at the end in the year 512 BC to his countryman, Timasitheos. The secret of his strength—as said by the texts of that time—lay in eating nine kilos of meat and nine of bread per day, well watered by nine liters of wine.

Another athlete, Diagoras of Rhodes, was one of the great boxers of the 5th century BC, but also the first of a family full of glory. He won the 79th edition of the Games and his three children and two of his grandchildren were Olympic champions too. In the 83rd edition, his firstborn Damagetos won in pancracy and the second, Akousilaos, in boxing. Upon returning to Rhodes, the boys entered the city carrying their father on their shoulders while a crazy crowd received them. Years later, the youngest of the brothers, Dorieus, won the pancracy in three consecutive games.

It is claimed that Melankomas of Caria (a city state of Asia Minor, present-day Turkey) won the boxing test of the 207 Olympiad without taking a single blow. Melankomas, a very agile man with an amazing speed of movement, used an unusual strategy that consisted of dodging the punchs of his opponents until they abandoned the fight due to exhaustion. His physical endurance was based on rigorous training. It is said that on one occasion he kept his arms extended for two full days, without lowering them or resting even for a single second.

COUBERTIN AND THE RESURRECTION

'Germany had exhumed the remains of Olympia. Why is France not going to get the revival of its splendour? From there to the project, less brilliant but more rapid and fruitful, of restoring the Olympic Games, there was only one step', because the time had come when the sport seemed to play its role in the world again.' The French nobleman Pierre de Frédy, baron of Coubertin—simply known as 'Pierre de Coubertin'—thus explained his enthusiasm to dig up the Olympic magnificence from the ruins of a Greek city. With great skill and pragmatism, in June 1894 Coubertin gathered in Paris representatives of sports movements from twelve countries (Argentina, Belgium, Austria-Bohemia, United States, Greece, Great Britain, Hungary, Italy, New Zealand, Russia, Sweden and, of course, France) to create the International Olympic Committee (IOC) and decree the first edition of the modern Olympic Games. 'His restoration was decided unanimously. We proposed to inaugurate them in 1900, but it was preferred to advance the date. It was decided that of 1896 and, at the proposal of Mr (Demetrius) Bikelas, Athens was designated as the place where the Games would be held for the first time', said the baron. Coubertin proved to have a good sense to take the reins of the brand new Olympic movement. Because of its history, the Games had to start in Greece, so he proposed that Bikelas be also the first president of the IOC, until the end of the inaugural competition. Then Coubertin would replace him and occupy the highest position for almost thirty years.

According to the French nobel, the founders of the brand new IOC unanimously agreed to 'place the (sports) competitions under the only patronage that could give them an aura of greatness and glory, that of the classical antiquity. To do this was to restore the Olympic Games. The name was imposed and it was not possible, in addition, to find another'.

ATHENS 1896

Fifteen centuries after the abolition ordered by the Roman emperor Theodosius I, the Games were reborn in Athens, thanks to the impulse of Pierre de Coubertin and the commitment of the entire Greek nation to dust off the glorious Olympics. Over ten days, from 6 April to 15 April 1896, runners, throwers, shooters, wrestlers, weightlifters, tennis players, swimmers, fenders and cyclists brightened each of the activities that opened a new era for the sport. It may be inevitable to compare this first 'modern' experience with the latest edition, Rio de Janeiro 2016, separated by 116 years. In Athens 1896, there were only 176 athletes from twelve nations, who performed in nine sports and forty-three disciplines. In Brazil there were 11,551 athletes from 206 countries, who played in twenty-eight competitions divided into 306 events. Although the contrast of the figures is overwhelming, it is essential to analyse the historical, cultural and even technological context in which the Olympics were held in Greece. At the end of the 19th century, without airplanes that shortened the times and distances, without sponsoring companies that collaborated with the necessary funds for the works, without television or radio, without advertising or promotion, Athens was a great achievement as the first venue of a new-era Olympic Game. Every great company was born from a small initiative, and if Rio 2016 was the greatest sporting success in history, with the participation of all the countries of the planet, it was undoubtedly possible due to the solid granite base chiseled by that first step in Athens. A small first step, perhaps not very firm(it is objected that no women or nations from Asia and Africa intervened),yet fundamental to begin a long and prosperous journey. The Greeks tried their best for the foundation of this innovative competition: the beautiful Panathenaic Stadium—the ruins of the old colosseum built in 350 BC were restored, thanks to the monetary contribution of the local rich businessman, George Averoff—dazzled in exquisite white marble from Mount Pentelicus. In addition to the contribution from Averoff, the organising committee, chaired by Prince Constantine, had to make a great effort to raise the necessary money to prepare all the stages. It even launched twelve special postal stamps, the first in history dedicated to sports. Only 16,000 series were released, which today have an incalculable value among collectors. For this edition it was decided to reward the winner of each event with a crown made with olive twigs and a silver medal. A bronze medal was reserved for the second and a diploma for the third. The realtively modern tradition of rewarding with gold, silver and bronze medals began in the third edition of the Games, in the US city of Saint Louis. In the statistical table elaborated with the current parameter, Greece was the country that added more medals, with 47 (in modern terms, 10 'gold', 18 'silver' and 19 'bronze'). However, the United States had the most winners (first prize holders): 11.

On 6 April 1896, before 50,000 spectators excited by the opening of the Olympics (so much enthusiasm was aroused by the Games that tickets were even resold), King George I of Greece decreed the return to life of the athletic competitions destined to promote peace and harmony between nations. Minutes after the official opening, the Panathenaic Stadium was the scene of the first tests. An American, called James Connolly, established himself as the first Olympic champion of the modern Games by easily winning the triple jump competition that culminated that same day. Connolly reached a record of 13.71 meters, 1 meter more than the second in the standings, Alexandre Tuffèri, a French national. The German gymnast Hermann Weingärtner was the athlete who won the most medals, with 6: 3 golds, 2 silver and 1 bronze, in the modern sense of the term. His compatriot, Carl Schuhmann added four golden hits, three in gymnastics and one in Greco-Roman wrestling. In the athletic field, there were notable doublets by the Americans—Thomas Burke (100 and 400 meters), Ellery Clark (high and long jump) and Bob Garrett (bullet and disc throw)—and the Australian Teddy Flack (800 and 1500 meters on track). However, the great hero of the first Games was an unknown local runner, Spyridon Louis, who only won one event. Of course, that was the marathon, the great event of the Olympiad.

THE MARATHON

For a tournament that gave life back to the Games, Coubertin wanted to incorporate into the program a new athletic competition that would be the culminating event of each Olympiad. After analysing different suggestions, the baron accepted a race devised by his friend and researcher, Michel Bréal. Bréal carefully reviewed the 'classic' Hellenic story and came up with the idea of recreating the epic of an Athenian soldier called Pheidippides, hero of the first of the three war clashes between the Greek city states and the Persian Empire during the 5th century BC.

According to the story of the historian Herodotus, at the end of the battle of Marathon, which defined the first Hellenic triumph, a hoplite named Pheidippides was summoned by his general, Miltiades, to run to Athens and report the victory over the Persians. The boy, already worn by the hard fight, stripped off his armor and ran to the city state, which was about 40 kilometers from the plain that had been the scene of the battle. Pheidippides jogged incessantly, and upon arrival, barely managed to announce the triumph: he died moments later because of the enormous effort.

One version says that the soldier died from a wound received during the battle and not from exhaustion, as he was used to carrying messages from Athens to Sparta, separated by about 160 kilometers. Another account argues that Pheidippides did not link Marathon with Athens, but with Sparta, over 200 kilometers, to request reinforcements. Beyond these discrepancies, Bréal proposed to Coubertin that the athletes follow the route between Marathon and Athens, through 42 kilometers. The idea really pleased the French nobleman, and marveled the Greeks. They were happy with a race baptised with the name of one of their localities that also paid tribute to one of their heroes.

However, keeping in mind the dark outcome of the 'original' race, what seemed great in the papers should be verified as doable in practice. First, two months before the start of the Games, two athletes were asked to run from the Marathon plain to the Greek capital to assess their performance. One of the volunteers dropped out in the middle of the test, but his partner managed to arrive safe about four hours after departure. Having passed the exam, the second step was to call a race to analyse its development: according to the British journalist Geoff Tibballs, on 10 March 1896, almost a month before the start of the Olympiad, the first marathon was held, with twelve participants, won by the Greek Charilaos Vasilakos with a time of 3 hours and 18 minutes. Two weeks later, the competition was repeated: Ioannis Laventis won a new world record of 3 hours, 11 minutes and 27 seconds. Another local runner named Spyridon Louis arrived seven minutes later, in fifth place. His time of glory would come on 10 April, when the novel race became, from morning to night, a famous contest aimed at immortalising its winner and placing it in the pantheon of the Olympic heroes, next to Pheidippides.

FIRST BOYCOTT

Not every country's absence in an edition of the Games can be considered a boycott. As such, it is understood exclusively as the act of pressure from one or several states—as can be observed throughout the Olympic history—to try to prevent or hinder the realisation of the sports tournament, as a means of coercion to make a claim heard or get a demand satisfied.

For the Athens Games, a single nation tried to boycott the event: the Ottoman Empire, constituted mainly by present-day Turkey, ancestral enemy of the Hellenics. In fact, Greece had become independent from the state of Asia Minor about sixty years ago, after remaining under its domination for about three and a half centuries, from the fall of Constantinople in 1453. No other nation joined the attempt to discredit the first edition of the modern games, so the Turks were the first and only boycotters.

PROTOCOL

Shortly after James Connolly recorded his name on the marble of sports history, the 100-meter dash playoffs began on the track. While preparing for the second qualifying series, an American named Thomas Curtis—who four days later would be champion in the 110-meter hurdles—was surprised to see that one of the participants of the first series, the French national, Alphonse Grisel, put on white gloves to face the competition. Why do you wear them?' Curtis asked. The Frenchman, after looking towards the official box where George I of Greece was, replied: 'Because I run in the presence of the king'. Grisel finished fourth that race—

behind the American natioanl, Francis Lane, the Hungarian national, Alajos Szokolyi and the British national, Charles Gmelin—and was eliminated. His particular interpretation of the protocol did not favour his aerodynamic capacity at all. It is said that, at the end of the race, the Frenchman assured Curtis that he would also intervene in the 400 meters, the discus throw, the long jump, parallel bars and the marathon. Stunned by such a variety of disciplines so different from each other, the American asked his colleague how to train for speed and long distance races at the same time. 'Well, it's very easy,' Grisel replied, 'one day I run a few meters very fast and the next day I run a greater distance very slowly'. Curtis was not surprised when, at the awards ceremony, the versatile French did not receive a single handshake. Without a doubt, Grisel deserved the medal of perseverance.

DISCUS THROWER

Princeton University student Robert Garrett had been designated to travel to Athens and participate in the shot-put event, a discipline in which he stood out as one of the bests in his country. But Garrett, a curious and restless guy, could not justify the very long trip to Greece to intervene exclusively in a single competition. For this reason, he asked his coaches to register him also in high jump, long jump and in an unknown event in the United States: discus throw. Garrett's proposal was taken almost as a joke, because nobody had the fundamental element to practise that discipline: the disc. However, the determined athlete said he would make one to arrive in Athens well prepared. Based on illustrations and engravings of ancient vessels, the twenty-year-old boy designed the strange artifact and commissioned a blacksmith friend to make it in steel. Following the same Hellenic drawings, he was rehearsing the appropriate movements to throw the instrument as far as possible. Thus, he practised for a week and embarked towards Greece. On 6 April, after the official opening of the Games, the discus throw was one of the first tests. When mixing with the other competitors, Garrett—the only American among three locals, two Danes, a British, a Swede and a Frenchman—discovered with surprise that the piece to throw was smaller and lighter than the one he had conceived: it was about 22 centimeters in diameter and 2 kilos of weight. Likewise, when he saw how his rivals practised, he felt ridiculous, since they all launched it from postures that imitated the classic sculpture *Discobolus* by the famous Athenian master Myron of Eleutherae. Far from being intimidated by so many 'novelties', including the rules he had to learn at the last minute, the American took his turn. His first two releases aroused laughter between his contestants and the public, for his clumsy movements and because the discus went anywhere. In fact, it almost caused a tragedy because it went close to falling among the spectators. However, on his third and final turn, Garrett turned himself on—in the style of the hammer throw—and threw the piece at 29 meters and 15 centimeters. His mark not only exceeded by 20 centimeters the best throw of his opponent, it also reached a world record. The day after his incredible feat, Garrett added another Olympic title in shot-put and went second in long jump. Four days later he would repeat the second place in high jump. With four medals, the improvised and surprising Discobolus returned home as the most successful American of the first edition of the modern Olympics.

THE YOUNGEST MEDALIST...KNOWN

Dimitrios Loundras was only 10 years and 218 days old when he participated in the Games as a component of the Greek gymnastics team on parallel bars. Member of the Ethnikos Gymnastikos Syllogos, the boy stood out for his skill and remarkable technique. On 9 April, thanks to the contribution of the small Loundras, his team finished in third place, which in the current tradition represents the 'bronze medal'.

Since that day, Dimitrios, who died in 1970, remains the youngest medalist in the Games. Actually, he is the smallest of the 'known'. In the following edition, Paris 1900, a boy who participated as a helmsman in a rowing event won the 'gold medal'. However, his identity and his true age—it is believed that he was seven or eight years old—continue to be an absolute mystery since then. This allowed the Greek to retain this novel title until now.

IN THE WINE THERE IS TRUTH, BUT…

Albin Lermusiaux had never run a distance as huge as the one proposed by the marathon. But excited by his third place in the 1500 meters, the intrepid Frenchman signed up himself in the new race that on 10 April closed the athletic competition in Athens. Lermusiaux planned a quick start to take the vanguard from the first moment, and then regulate the forces to get a final sprint in the last meters. The test began and the Frenchman, as he had calculated, placed himself at the forefront. Slowly, the kilometers were left behind, always with the Frenchman in the lead. Only 8 kilometers from the stadium, the triumph of Lermusiaux seemed a fact. However, destroyed by fatigue and thirst, which had begun to affect his resistance, the runner who headed the race accepted a couple of glasses of wine offered by a spectator on the side of the road. The French drank with great content and returned to the competition, but immediately noticed that something was wrong: alcohol, quickly absorbed by his empty stomach, mixed with exhaustion in a lethal cocktail that exploded in his head. Lermusiaux collapsed and had to be helped by some of the neighbours who looked curiously at the corridors. Although he soon returned to himself, the Frenchman could not take another step. One of his assistants recalled an old sentence of the Greek poet Alcaeus of Mytilene:

In the wine there is truth; but in the water, health.

THE GREAT CHAMPION

After the desertions of Flack and Lermusiaux, the lead of the race was a local athlete: Spyridon Louis. He was a twenty-three-year-old boy born in the town of Marousi, north of Athens, who used to work as a waterman, carrying buckets. The Greek had also drunk wine offered by the spectators to quench the flames of thirst, but with a result diametrically opposed to that of the Frenchman, strengthened by the nectar of grapes, he ran nonstop to the stadium. Fifty thousand people burst into shouts of joy and loud applause when they discovered that this little athlete advancing alone on the track towards the finishing line was their countryman. The excitement was such that the Princes Constantine and George jumped from the official box to join Louis, one on each side, till the end. Though they later assured that they had done it to protect the corridor from any eventual incident. At the feet of Louis, flowers, money, jewelery and hats fell from the stands to reward such remarkable action. The winner, who cut the arrival belt after 2 hours, 58 minutes and 50 seconds of intense jogging, went, as if by magic, from an unknown athlete to a national hero. His victory earned him all kinds of awards, from small fortunes gathered by newspapers, clubs and politicians, to haircuts and free food supplies for life. Perhaps the most succulent reward was offered by the potent George Averoff: the hand of his daughter in marriage, and a dowry of one million drachmas, the same amount that had cost the Panathinaiko. Louis thanked the generous proposal of the businessman, but had to reject it because he was already married and had two children. His response was different when, during the awards ceremony, King George I asked him what he would like to receive to celebrate his feat. The champion, a simple and humble man, did not hesitate: 'A cart with two oxen to help me carry water'.

THE FIRST MARATHON CHEAT

About six minutes behind Spyridon Louis, another Greek runner, Kharilaos Vasilakos arrived at the stadium. Soon arrived Spyridon Velokas, a third local athlete. In the fourth place arrived the first foreigner: the Hungarian Gyula Kellner. However, as soon as he caught his breath, the Hungarian denounced that Velokas had resorted to a ploy during the race. According to Kellner, the Greek had climbed into a horse-drawn carriage to cover a significant portion of the route. The organisers questioned Velokas, who repenting, confessed the scam. He was immediately disqualified. During the awards ceremony, King George I gave the Hungarian a gold watch as compensation for the bad time.

GOLDEN TOURIST

In 1894, the Irishman John Boland invited his Greek friend Thrasyvoalos Manaos to speak at a congress on sports held at the University of Oxford. Manaos, a member of a powerful Hellenic family, was very grateful for the invitation, and two years later, after being appointed member of the organising committee of the Olympiad, he wanted to pay back Boland's gesture and called him up to be a witness of the first modern Games. Upon arriving in the Greek capital, the Irish noted that the Olympic calendar included a tennis tournament, one of his favourite sports, and decided to participate in it. In his first game at the Lawn Tennis in Athens, Boland beat German national, Friedrich Traun. Then, he defeated the Greeks, Evangelos Rallis and Konstantinos Paspatis in quarter-finals and semi-finals, respectively. On 11 April, in the finals, the Irish beat local player Dimitrios Kasdaglis. But his feat did not end there: Traun had been very impressed by the quality of Boland, and invited him to intervene in the doubles contest, because his partner had been injured. The Irish accepted and the 'duo' (at that time teams with players of different nationalities were allowed) went on to win gold after beating two Greek teams: Aristidis and Konstantinos Akratopoulos, first, and Demetrios Petrokokkinos and Kasdaglis, in the last game. Thus, the man who had arrived in Athens as a tourist returned to his homeland as a double Olympic champion.

SWIMMER, JOKER AND ARCHITECT

As there were no appropriate pools in Athens for swimming events, the organisers of the Games determined that the three races—100, 400 and 1200 meters—would take place at sea in the Bay of Zea, attached to the port of Athens, the Piraeus. This decision, of course, implied a problem: nobody could ensure that the waters of the Aegean would be calm on the day set for the competitions. And unfortunately, on the morning of Sunday, 12 April, the sea woke up very rough, with high waves and very frozen water. Despite the adverse conditions, the organisers decided to move on, and for the first race, six brave participants were taken by boat to a platform from which they dived and fought against the waves to return to the mainland. The winner was the Hungarian national, Alfred 'Hajos' Guttmann, an eighteen-year-old architecture student who had learned to swim at thirteen, after his father drowned in the Danube river.

The sea calmed down a little for the next test, the 1200 meters. Three boats moved the six contestants to the platform. Before the start shot, two of the boats returned to the pier and one remained to act in case of any contingency. Guttmann, who had suffered the low water-temperature in the first race, smeared his body with fat to protect himself from the cold. Regardless of this armor, he decided to leave in the middle beset by a cramp. But, to his surprise, the relief boat was still further than the finishing line, so he continued swimming to save his life. His survival instinct not only allowed him to beat the danger, but to win the meet with a time of 18:22.2. 'My biggest fight was against the waves—they reached a height of 4 meters that morning—and the water was terribly cold', said the champion, who surpassed the Greek Joannis Andreou by 2.5 minutes.

During the banquet of honour for the Olympic champions, King George I of Greece approached Guttmann respectfully and asked him where he had learned to swim so well. 'In the water,' the Hungarian replied, trying to be funny. The disgraceful sense of humour did not last for the young swimmer: when he returned exultantly to his classes at the University of Budapest, happy that his name appeared prominently in all newspapers, Guttmann was reprimanded without mercy by the dean of his faculty for having been absent several weeks without authorisation. 'Your medals do not interest me. I am eager to hear your answers in your next exam,' the teacher intimidated him, ignoring his sport fame. The Olympic champion took the degree seriously and in a few years, graduated with honours.

PARIS 1900

A maxim attributed to Napoleon Bonaparte—possibly adapted from a Chinese proverb—argues that sometimes it is necessary to go back two steps to advance one. Paris 1900 and St. Louis 1904 were, in some way, two unavoidable negative strides that contributed, finally, to consolidate the notable Olympic history. The Paris Games failed even before its beginning because Pierre de Coubertin had to grant that the sports event was part of the Universal Exhibition Program that, during 1900, was held in the Fields of Mars, at the foot of the novel Eiffel Tower, and in numerous parks, museums, palaces and theaters of the French capital. Since it was part of a major event, this Olympiad was the only one that had no opening or closing ceremony exclusively. In addition, the competitions extended about six months, and most of the foreign participants left Paris ignorant that the tournaments in which they had participated corresponded to the second edition of the Games. Many believed that it was a sports celebration linked to the exhibition. The athletic events were carried out in the Boulogne Forest, a park located west of the city, with the corresponding authorisation from the Parisian town hall. However, the permit did not allow the pruning of trees or the installation of an athletic track of volcanic ashes—the 'official' surface of that time—so that the different sports scenarios could be adapted to the beautiful landscape of the promenade. And quite naturally, it resulted in numerous irregularities. As there was not a corresponding budget, the trace was marked directly on the grass, and sand and sawdust were added. For hurdle races, telephone posts were used as obstacles. Another Coubertin concession was to accept that the program included unusual tests, such as a fishing contest in the Seine, which paradoxically gathered more spectators than the rest of the sports. Disciplines such as polo, cricket, croquet, golf and tug-of-war were also incorporated, which currently are no longer part of the program. In terms of its orgianisation, there were also failures and disagreements. The German delegation, for example, had to spend their first Parisian night on the street and sleep under the stars, because they had not reserved rooms in a hotel. Hard blows also came from Athens: the competition arranged for the first time outside Greece was strongly questioned by the Hellenics. A newspaper in the Greek capital said that 'Mr Coubertin is a thief who wants the Games to be held in cities that are not Greek. This is how he steals one of our most precious jewels: the Olympics'.

Despite all this, Paris 1900 had, of course, many positive aspects: the most relevant being perhaps the participation of women. Twenty-three women broke Coubertin's misogynistic wall and dared to compete in tennis, golf and croquet. The British national Charlotte Cooper became the first lady to be Olympic champion beating the French national, Hélène Prévost, in the individual tennis final. In addition, the intervening countries increased from twelve to twenty-nine, and athletes, from 176 to 1224. The famous medals were not yet delivered, but for the official records of the IOC, the championis considered as winner of 'gold', the ruuner up as of 'silver' and the first runner up as winner of 'bronze' in each discipline. According to this method, France, with 104, was the country that won the most awards (27 golds, 40 silvers and 37 coppers), followed by the United States, with 47 (19 golds).

Football, the most popular sport in the world, was first included in an Olympiad in this edition, although the tournament was an exhibition with three clubs from England, Belgium and France.

ILLUSION OF THE GAME

According to the book *History of the Olympic Games* by John Kieran and Arthur Daley, the athletes who represented the United States in the track and field tests 'had no idea that they were playing the second Olympiad until they received their medals, when they finished the competition. They thought they were only part of an international meeting included in the Paris Exhibition that year. Upon receiving their medals, they were informed that their names had been registered as Olympic champions'. The program, in fact, pointed out: 'French Republic, Universal Exhibition of 1900. International Championships. Foot races and amateur athletic competitions organized by the Union of French Athletic Sports Societies'. No reference to the Games.

While studying art in Paris, an American student, Margaret Abbott, read in a newspaper that a nine-hole women's golf tournament would be held at the Compiègne Golf Club, located about 30 kilometers north of the city. Abbott signed up and competed against nine other women, four from the USA and five French. The art student completed the course in 47 strokes and won by 2 ahead of her compatriot Polly Whittier, who was second. The American Daria Pratt also completed the podium, with 53 strokes. Abbott received as a prize a beautiful porcelain vase with details in carved gold. All her life she believed that she had won a local contest. She died in 1955 in the city of Greenwich, Connecticut, without anyone ever announcing that her name had been chiseled on the Olympic marble.

MOTORS

The Olympic regattas were scheduled at a bend in the legendary Seine, between the towns of Meulan and Les Mureaux, located northwest of Paris. The most important test was the 'Open Class', which gathered 47 sailboats, 43 of them French. However, the morning of 20 May 1900 was presented without a drop of wind, which turned the race into a real fiasco. For hours, the boats remained immobilised on the waters, with their thin sails unmoved. Finally, when a light breeze took pity on the bored sailors, only six of the intervening sailboats were still determined to reach the finishing line: the rest had preferred to return to land to enjoy a good glass of red wine. The British ship Scotia won the 'gold' after almost six hours of slow travel, followed by the German Aschenbrodel and the French Turquoise-1. Then two other local vessels, Carabinier and Mamie, arrived. But when the docking officers discovered that both had steam engines for their propulsion, their names were immediately scrapped off from the official record.

CHAMPION BY ACCIDENT

Denmark's Edgar Aaybe was not a great athlete. In fact, he did not travel to Paris as an athlete, but as a journalist to cover the Olympic for the newspaper *Politiken*. On 16 July, while circling aimlessly through the Boulogne forest, Aaybe met his countrymen Charles Winckler, who had not qualified for the final disc and bullet throws, and Eugen Schmidt. Noting that the reporter was big and seemed to be quite strong, Schmidt and Winckler invited him to join the 'mixed' tug-of-war team along with three other Swede boys, as they needed an extra competitor to face the tough contenders of the Paris Racing Club. The journalist accepted the invitation and joined the Scandinavian group. His contribution was essential to win the fight against the locals. As the duel was the only one in that specialty—only two teams had signed up for that event—Aaybe proudly returned home with his unexpected Olympic champion title.

ABANDONMENT AND TRIUMPH

On 22 July, the athletic events culminated in a strange race: the 5000-meter track for teams. This competition—actually a 'face-to-face' duel between two institutions, the local racing club and the British Amateur Athletic Association—consisted of a race with five participants per group, each of whom received a score according to their order of arrival, from first to tenth. The qualification by athlete allowed that, in practice, the test had an incredible result: the team that won…did not finish the race! How was this possible? Because English Alfred Tysoe, Charles Bennett, Jack Rimmer and Sidney Robinson reached the finishing line before the five Frenchmen, which added enough points for the Amateur Athletic Association to win the contest. The triumph was crystallised despite the fifth member of the British team, the Australian Stanley Rowley—who had already won three 'bronzes' in the 60, 100 and 200 meters—never completed his part. Rowley suffered a muscle contracture during the competition that forced him first to limp, then just to walk overwhelmed by pain. The test officials, seeing that the British team had already collected enough points to obtain the 'gold', and that all the French had completed the 5000 meters, took pity on the poor Australian and allowed him to leave when he had barely covered half the distance. Rowley, in this way, reached the curious privilege of being an Olympic champion in a race he had given up. For its poor call and his unusual final, the 5000 meters per team never again became part of the Games calendar.

FIRE AND BLOOD

It is very difficult to speculate the reason behind putting the Olympic shooting calendar into this edition. One of the credible reasons is perhaps, due to the Universal Exhibition in Paris, many arms manufacturers organised public contests at their exhibition stands.

There were also tournaments where cash prizes were awarded, which immediately turned their winners into 'professional' athletes. A really spine-chilling statistic confirms that, in total, there were forty different competitions, with 6351 shooters and 5,18,602 shots taken.

Probably the most bloodthirsty event at the foot of the Eiffel Tower was the 'pigeon shooting', which the Belgian national, Léon de Lunden won after killing twenty-one birds. It is estimated that this event left an amount of 300 dead pigeons.

SWEET WATER

In Athens, swimming contests took place in a 'natural' environment: a bend in the River Seine bordering the town of Asnières-sur-Seine. Between 11 and 12 August, seven contestants, all male, were dropped in a 'pool' bounded by boats, ropes and buoys. The curious thing about the program was that, along with the normal races such as the 200-, 1000- and 4000-meter freestyle, absurd competitions were included, such as '60 meters under water'. In this crazy competition, only two of the fourteen contestants were able to meet the objective: the rest had to surface to avoid drowning. Frenchman Charles de Vendeville won gold with a time of 1: 08.4, three seconds less than his compatriot André Six. However, the greatest madness consisted of a '200 meters with obstacles' test, which forced swimmers to pass under barrels. This competition, more typical of a circus than of an Olympiad, was won by the Australian Frederick Lane, who had also triumphed in the 200-meter free style.

GOLDEN AND IGNORED

The town of Asnières-sur-Seine also hosted the rowing events, which had its debut at the Games since previously it had to be suspended due to bad weather in Athens. On 25 August, when the preliminaries of couples with helmsman were made, the Dutch François Antoine

Brandt and Roelof Klein were not satisfied with their performance. Although they had qualified for the final, they had been widely surpassed by the boat of the Société Nautique de la Marne, who carried a child as helmsman. Similarly, the boats of two other French rowing institutions—Rowing Club Castillon and Cercle Nautique de Reims—carried one boy each as a guide. They, on the other hand, had been assisted by their compatriot Hermanus Gerardus Brockmann, who was a twenty-eight-year-old *boy*, much larger and heavier. That night, Brandt and Klein agreed that, in order to have a chance to win the competition, they had to replace their partner with a young boy who lost kilos to his boat, named Minerva Amsterdam. The next day, the Dutch searched between the assistants until they found a French boy who had reached the shore as a spectator with his parents, whom they invited to join their team. The boy, permitted by his dad and also by the judges of the event, boarded the boat and quickly understood what his task would be. Perfectly complemented and much lighter, the Dutch team improved a great performance and became champion for a hair over the representatives of the Société Nautique de la Marne. After hugging and being congratulated by Brockmann, who had followed the race from a pier, Brandt and Klein wanted to invite their young helper to drink something refreshing, but they noticed that the boy had disappeared moments after setting his feet on solid ground, just like his family. For the official IOC registration, the victory corresponded to a 'mixed team', because the crew of the winning boat were two Dutch men and one French. The only thing that was not inscribed in the Olympic record was the name of the rookie athlete. Although he could never prove his identity or his precise age—it is speculated that he was seven or eight years old. Historians agree that the unknown boy is the youngest champion in the history of the Games.

SAINT LOUIS 1904

Like Paris 1900, the St Louis Games also proved to be a stain on the famous White collar of the Olympic history. Among many other mistakes made by the organisers, the main ones were the very idea of joining a new World Fair, with a very extended calendar (from 1 July to 23 November); allowing the fixation of some ridiculous events; the almost absence of foreign athletes, with the consequent transformation of an olympiad into a tournament between universities and American clubs; and in some competitions, replacing the metric system by the Anglo-Saxon (miles, yards and feet), that modified the distances significantly and prevented the logical record of records. But the most blunderous one was to have included in the calendar the 'Anthropological Days', a humiliating exhibition of human beings of different ethnicities in a kind of 'zoo of people', with the aggravating display of activities more typical of circus than of sport. In fact, these Olympics failed even before the first whistle was given, thanks to the absence of the President of the IOC, Pierre de Coubertin, who refused to travel to the United States to be part of that bizarre spectacle.

Of the 96 gold medals at stake, the host country won 75. In some sports, such as boxing—which debuted at the Games—only local fighters intervened. This made it easier for the host team to obtain the historical record of medals: 230. Probably because of the great distances that Europeans should undertake, only the 10 per cent of the 650 athletes belonged to other countries, and many of them had traveled months before as immigrants and they were working in the different pavilions of the World Fair. In the sports field, improvised disciplines such as sexatlon were presented—which had three gymnastics tests (colt, bar and parallels) and three athletics (100 meters, long jump and shot-put)—and there were baseball exhibitions, lacrosse, croquet and its roque variant, football and basketball. Swimming took place in an artificial lake that was fed by a river near the site where the Universal Fair was held. The waterbody was bounded by boats and buoys.

Of course, the third Olympic edition also had positive facts: the most important was the incorporation of today's traditional custom of delivering gold, silver and bronze medals to the champions, the second and third, respectively, of each competition.

NO ANTHROPOLOGY

The organisers of the infamous World Fair—all white people—solved the equation easily. On one hand, the Olympic Games were not fun enough. They considered that an event was needed that could make the spectators laugh who were less interested in the races and jumps. On the other hand, the United States had already become a country that summoned immigrants of the most diverse ethnicities, and the event had attracted like a magnet the needy workers from the most distant parts of the globe. With so much 'workforce' available, the Anthropology emerged, which had little to do with the study of human reality. Aboriginal African and American, Chinese, Moors and Syrians dressed in their traditional dresses gave life to a kind of zoo of people. As in an animal circus, 'specimens' were forced to eat monkeys and other exotic foods, and to participate in contests of weight-throwing and other activities in which they were shown in ridiculous situations.

The tasteless ending was a fighting tournament that, in the best style of a Roman Colosseum, faced disparate-looking people, like a black giant against two pygmies. Incomprehensibly, this sad fact generated guffaws in the audience. When Coubertin learned what had happened, he described the exhibition as 'an outrageous fact', typical of 'a young country', but warned that 'when these blacks, these coppers and these yellows learn to run, jump, throw, they will leave whites behind them'. He was not wrong.

BEWARE OF THE DOG

Len Tau and Jan Mashiani arrived in the United States proud to be the first Africans to compete in an Olympiad. The young people, students of the University of the Free State of South Africa, were two fast aboriginal runners of the Tswana Kafs tribe who had intervened as messengers in the second Boer Wars, which faced the British imperialists and the colonisers. After introducing themselves to the organisers of the Games, Tau and Mashiani were forced to dress with feathers and rags and participate as Zulus in the humiliating 'Anthropological Days'. The officers told them that if they were not part of that farce, they could not run the marathon, the contest for which they had traveled. Overcome with the humiliating moment, on 30 August the two boys showed up at Francis Field to intervene in the 40-kilometer race. The South Africans started in a good position, and little by little Tau was consolidated as one of the candidates for the gold medal. When he had a few kilometers to reach the finishing line and fatigue began to deteriorate his resistance, a huge rabid dog came out of a small grove along the road and advanced furiously towards the young African. When he realised that the beast was approaching to him, throwing foam and with clear intentions to nail its affiliated teeth, Tau forgot about fatigue and the race and escaped at full speed through a cornfield. After walking almost a kilometer among the cobs, the South African checked that he had eluded the fierce animal, returned to the road and resumed the competition with great determination. Tau reached the finishing line in ninth place, almost half an hour after the winner, the local Tom Hicks. He returned to South Africa without medals, but at least he did not add sharp fangs to his luggage.

THE TREACHEROUS APPLES

The message on the shirt aroused the curiosity of the neighbors of Havana. 'Support for a Cuban athlete', it claimed with a hand-drawn typeface. When someone dared to interrogate Felix 'Andarin' ('Walker') Carvajal for more details, there was no turning back. The charisma and the unparalleled lips of the friendly long-distance runner enveloped the question until he got a coin or a bill to help to pay for the dream trip to Saint Louis. Gradually, but without pause, Carvajal reached his first objective: gather enough money to travel to the Games. Unfortunately, after crossing the Gulf of Mexico, the alcohol, the perfidious women and the New Orleans dice were plotted to leave him without a penny. However, far from being frightened, the boy showed that his Olympic enthusiasm remained firm, and completed walking and hitchhiking the 1100 kilometers that separate the famous jewel of the Mississippi of St Louis.

Although he arrived at the Washington University campus with no money or healthy shoes, his warm personality soon won everyone's friendship: fonded by the cuban charisma, a group of American weightlifters got him some food and a place to sleep. Another athlete gave him a pair of used boots; a third, a pair of shirts and pants. On 30 August, when 'Andarin' appeared at Francis Field, he didn't look as a sportsman with his makeshift outfit. The weightlifter Martin Sheridan, with scissors, cut the sleeves of the pants and shirts so that the Cuban could move more easily during the long race. He also slashed the reeds of his boots, although nothing could be done to lighten his thick heavy soles.

At the beginning of the contest, the Caribbean threw himself at the vanguard and remained between the front bunch during the first half. But little by little hunger became a lethal enemy. Starving and without any help, Carvajal decided to stop and take the juicy fruits of an apple tree that stood on the side of the road. With his stomach full, the Cuban returned with renewed impetus to the competition. But his spirit soon ran into another incident: the apples, which were not yet ripe enough, caused a sudden and intense diarrhea that forced a 'technical stop' behind a nearby pasture. Yet almost ignoring the new inconvenience, 'Andarín' continued in his way and he was very close to winning a medal: he reached the finishing line in fourth place, just ten minutes after the third, the local Arthur Newton. What he did get was an exciting reception from the public, which celebrated his self-esteem with an enormous applause.

CHEATERS

Enthused by the illusion of being the first American to win an Olympic marathon, Frederick Lorz left the Francis Field at full speed, convinced that if he occupied the vanguard he could keep it until the end. Of course, little accustomed to this type of long-breath racing, Lorz had to leave after the first 10 kilometers, completely exhausted. On the edge of fainting, the racer agreed to get into a Ford car, a novelty at that time, which accompanied the contest as an exhibition and it was heading towards Washington University. The ride revitalised Lorz. Recovered, he got out of the vehicle a few kilometers from the goal ('I have to pick up my things,' he said to the driver) and continued running. Upon entering the stadium, the opportunist athlete was greeted with a standing ovation by the thousands of fans waiting for the definition of the prestigious race. He not only cut the arrival ribbon and celebrated as if he had won in good law, but also took a picture with the daughter of the then president Theodore Roosevelt. After countless displays of affection, Lorz said he felt tired and retired to the locker room, where he changed and disappeared. When the organisers of the Games discovered the fraud mounted by the alleged winner, they disqualified him and demanded that the athletic association punish him with a lifelong ban. However, the penalty extended for just one year, after which Lorz demonstrated his true skills as a runner by winning the traditional Boston marathon.

Another cheater-winner was Thomas Hicks, an Englishman enrolled for the arduous contest as an American. During the long race, the British was twice ready to leave because of the enormous effort. However, on those two occasions he was assisted by a supposed coach who injected him strychnine—a central nervous system-stimulating alkaloid, which in excess can cause seizures, respiratory failures and brain death—in view of the spectators and even the judges of the test. The collaborator also offered him to have an egg yolk and cognac shake. Some participants denounced these irregularities to the organisers, but Hicks was legitimised as a champion despite having collapsed after crossing the finishing line, and suffered hallucinations during the awards ceremony in which he could not even stand. On his way home, the English vanished while sitting in the trolley, and only came back when an employee woke him up at the terminal. The case pushed the IOC to begin taking the first precautions against doping. The doctors consulted later told that Hicks would have died if his assistant applied a third dose of strychnine.

THE STRANGE CASE OF OLIVER KIRK

The people who filled the Physical Culture Gymnasium of Washington University was not satisfied on a Thursday, 22 September. It seemed unfair to the audience that Frank Haller be rewarded without having fought that same afternoon. Haller had knocked out Frederick Gilmore on Wednesday in the only featherweight match—just two contestants had signed up—and had appeared on campus the next day to receive his gold medal. But the spectators who had not attended on Wednesday wanted to see him in action. After several discussions, Haller agreed to fight with Oliver Kirk, favoured by a double advantage: Kirk had fought a while before (he had won over George Finnegan by knockout) and belonged to the bantamweight category, several kilos lower than his opponent. However, inside the quadrilateral, Haller's supposed superiority was not confirmed. Kirk surpassed him widely, and although he failed to finish the duel by knock out, he was declared the winner by unanimous decision. Thus, the champion achieved a record never equaled: two gold boxing medals in two different categories in the same Game. Although it is objected that he played only two fights, one in bantamweight and one in featherweight, the truth is that everything was resolved in a single day. When he moved to the professional level, Kirk also won two victories, but then he wove an unfortunate series of eight losses. Bruised, the record-man preferred to step aside. He had already reaped enough glory.

BASKET

Just twelve years after being created by the Canadian James Naismith, basketball arrived at the Games, although as an exhibition sport. According to the records, only five teams intervened: Buffalo German YMCA, Missouri AC, Chicago Central YMCA, Xavier AC and Turner Tigers. Buffalo became champion after beating Chicago in the final by 39 to 28. At the same time, there were competitions between primary, secondary and university school teams, all from the United States. This sport would be officially added to the Olympic calendar much later for the 1936 Berlin Games.

THE CHAMPION OF THE WOODEN LEG

On 2 July, a particular triathlon was developed at Francis Field that combined long jump, bullet shooting and a 100-yard run. One of its participants was George Eyser, a thirty-two-year-old man who was born in Kiel, Germany, but was a US national since he was fourteen years old and lived in St Louis. Eyser's performance was very weak, to the point of finishing last among 118 athletes. However, the newspapers of the time highlighted his performance because the German, who had lost his left leg as a child in a railway accident, ran with a wooden prosthesis.

On 28 October, when the gymnastics tests were held, Eyser again competed with his stick limb and achieved a diametrically opposite result: he won the gold medal in rope climbing, vault and parallel bars, silver in pommel horse and combined exercises and bronze in horizontal bar. With a total of six medals in the same Olympiad, Eyser starred in one of the most exciting performances in history.

LONDON 1908

The 1908 Games had originally been assigned to Rome, but the eruption of Vesuvius volcano, which occurred on 7 April 1906, disrupted the plans of the 'Eternal City'. The Italian government had to give up the Olympiad and use all its financial resources to overcome the serious consequences caused by the phenomenon in the Campagnia region, especially in front of the Bay of Naples. For this contingency, London offered to take the Roman baton, a proposal enthusiastically received by the IOC. In just two years, the British capital invested huge sums to build a new stadium, called White City, with a capacity of 80,000 spectators, the first Olympic swimming pools that allowed world records to be destroyed in all the competitions, and refit all sports and hotel facilities that already existed. The leaders of the IOC feared at first that the event would be linked to a fair again, in this case the Franco–British show. However, the development of sports events remained outside the exhibition and developed quite normally, although the various disciplines were carried out in a very wide period from April to October. In terms of the organisation, the religious problems of Paris 1900 were taken into account, so that, to avoid new controversies, no competitions were scheduled on Sunday.

In the general positions table, the United Kingdom took full advantage of its host status to add the largest number of medals—146, of which 56 were golds—and be the first nation for the only time in the Olympic history. Of course, the victory of the home team had some 'little help' because many sports included in the official calendar were almost unknown at that time outside the islands, such as rackets, in wich the Union Jack flag occupied all the places on the podium. Several controversial decisions of the judges and referees, all of British nationality, also helped the locals. The IOC took note of the few disagreed and proposed to modify the issue for the next edition.

A unique fact in the awards ceremonies was that only the men received medals: the winning women were awarded with an unfair diploma instead of badges.

At the Prince's Skating Club in Knightsbridge, ice skating competitions were first held, something unusual for a summer Olympiad. This discipline (which included four tests: two male, one mixed and one female) would be back in Antwerp 1920, but from 1924 it would become part of the Winter Games calendar. Another sport that had a curious proposal was tennis: two parallel tournaments were scheduled, one on outdoor courts and another on covered courts. This would be repeated only in Stockholm 1912, and both the Games ended without any player getting the title in the two specialties.

The Olympic football tournament organised in the British capital was the first in which national teams competed officially. The home team was left with the gold after beating the Danish squad by 2 to 0 in the final because of the singular fact: referee John Lewis and his two linesmen were all English.

ROYAL CAPRICE

The official distance of the marathon was consolidated in this Olympic edition, thanks to a real caprice. After, rather, two caprices. The organisers of the Games had planned a 40-kilometer journey that ended at the

White City Stadium. But to satisfy King Edward VII, the race extended 2 kilometers to the walls of Windsor Castle, located west of London. The monarch wanted his daughter Mary, who had been a mother hours before and was resting in her room, to see the corridors leaving from her window. The measure was modified again on the same day of the race, on 24 July, while the athletes approached to the colosseum. Due to the rain that fell on the English capital, the local Olympic committee agreed to move the finishing line half a turn to the track (exactly 195 meters) to the base of the official box, so that Eduardo VII and the rest of his royal family could enjoy the resolution of the competition without getting wet. In this way, the 42 kilometers 195 meters were reflected in the Olympic records and consolidated as the official marathon distance forever. It all goes back to the eccentricities of the British king and his aristocratic clan.

GOLDEN GRANDFATHER

On 9 July, the Bisley Rifle Range was the scene of the debut of the Olympic 'grandfather', the Swedish Oscar Swahn. Expert shooter, always accompanied by his son Alfred, Swahn won that day his first gold medal in the specialty 'running deer shooting-single shot', at the age of sixty. Before leaving London, the Swede hung on his chest another gold in the same specialty, although in teams, and a bronze also in mobile target, double shot. Four years later, in Stockholm, the Swede, sixty-four years, was established as the oldest Olympic champion by repeating gold in the 'deer' team contest, with his son. Until that time, the golden longevity title belonged to British Joshua Millner, who had won the '1000-yard rifle' event at the age of sixty-one in London. In his own land, Swahn was fifth in the individual category, which coincidentally was won by his son Alfred. After the First World War, Oscar traveled to Antwerp 1920 Games when he turned seventy-two and not only got the silver—

again in ‘running deer shooting-single shot’, again with his son—but crystallised a triple title that remains unchanged: the oldest champion (sixty-four years), medalist and participant (both at seventy-two years) in the history of the Games.

HE WON BUT HE WAS NOT THE CHAMPION

Many times, throughout the different editions of the Games, it happened that the winner of a contest did not finally receive the gold medal, or received it and then had to return it. The majority of these cases happened after an irregularity observed by the judges, or that the athlete tested positive in the doping test. But what happened on 11 July in the Bisley Rifle Range in London, however, was altogether a different thing, more typical of Ripley: a shooter, in addition to getting the best performance, broke the world record, but was not awarded with gold for the late arrival of a partner. How do you explain this strange case, unique in the Olympic history?

The ‘small-bore rifle’ contest allowed each country to present a maximum of twelve competitors. The only team that completed its official list was the local one, Great Britain. However, when the judges ordered the start of the event—which consisted of a tour of various targets—the team captain exploded: one of his stars and a medal candidate, George Barnes, had forgotten his identity documents. Given the possibility of wasting one of the places, the leader team summoned Philip Plater, who had been called as a substitute. When Plater was already in the middle of his involvement, a relative of Barnes appeared in the polygon with the identification papers. Before the controversy, the captain decided that Barnes, owner of a better record than Plater, would participate and the substitute’s results be annulled. When the reserve contestant finished his round, he was informed of the decision taken by the squad manager and how futile his effort had been. Plater left the pavilion indignantly: he had added 391 points, a new world record. The official winner, Arthur Carnell, had only 387, and Barnes, who finished third, 285. The informal champ was rewarded shortly thereafter with a gold medal and a special diploma from the British Olympic Committee. However, these awards were not enough to overcome the pain of his notable 'non-approved' performance and the disappearance of his name from the official Olympic records. In England Plater is perhaps the most unfortunate athlete in history.

BAD DRINK

'What can be better than a traditional English beer to celebrate the qualificationfor the final 1500-meter race?', thought the French Alexandre François Étienne Jean Bouin (better known as Jean Bouin) the afternoon of 13 July, when he left the White City Stadium. Thirsty for a foamy beer that would gratify his effort and relax his spirit, Bouin went straight to a pub in Soho, in the center of the English capital. The first delicious pint seemed not good enough and was soon followed by another, and another. Filled with abundant fermented barley and with the doughy tongue, the guy from Marseille got entangled in an argument with two local sailors, which began with issues in sports and finished in a new sport: boxing. The uproar, which included the throwing of glasses and chairs, could only be contained after the appearance of several agents of the rigid London Police. Expressed by two uniformed big men, Bouin tried to detach himself from the mess, first denouncing his rivals, then with apologies and finally invoking his Olympic athlete status, but there was no way to elude his way to an uncomfortable cell.

The next day, when the French managers discovered the absence of the runner on the track, they began an arduous journey through hotels and hospitals, until the quarrelsome Bouin was found behind the bars of a police station. Thanks to the intervention of the officers' delegation, the athlete regained freedom but too late for the contest: the American Mel Sheppard had already won it. Bouin did have time, after the reprimand of his official, to join four other companions with whom, that same afternoon, he participated in the preliminary of the 3-mile team race. France eliminated Sweden, qualified and, the next morning, won the bronze medal behind Great Britain and the United States. Bouin celebrated his prize with a delicious glass of mineral water.

BURSTED BY BUBBLES

Charles Hefferon was born in the English town of Berkshire, but became a South African national after intervening in the Boer War, which ended in 1902, and accepted a job as a guard officer in a prison. In his new homeland, Hefferon began to compete in long-distance races, thanks to his remarkable resistance. Enthused by his results and advised by his new compatriots, the runner decided to travel to the British capital to participate in two contests: the 5-mile race—an event discontinued after Athens 1906 and London 1908—and the marathon. In the first competition, the performance of the South African was good, although not good enough to get him a medal: Hefferon qualified for the final of 18 July, but arrived at the finishing line in the fourth place.

On 24 July, the guard showed up at Windsor Castle, where the marathon starting line was established to satisfy his triumphant desire. After the initial shot, Hefferon flew as an arrow and immediately placed himself in front of the competition. With a firm and fast stride, the South African led the race for more than 40 kilometers. Only 1500 meters from the finishing line, Hefferon stopped to accept a glass of champagne held by one of the members of the public on the side of the road. The oversight was fatal to the leader: while he drank and was hugged and congratulated by some spectators, he was surpassed by two of his rivals, the Italian Dorando Pietri and the American John Hayes.

Hefferon returned desperate to the race, but the fatigue and the short distance remaining did not allow him to discount the disadvantage. The South African completed the marathon in 2 hours, 56 minutes and 6 seconds, 2 minutes more than the Italian and 48 seconds behind the American. While bronze was later transformed into silver, by Pietri's disqualification, Hefferon regreted his blunder. The glass of champagne had cost him too much .

WITHOUT GOLD

Italian pastry chef Dorando Pietri didn't know where he was. His legs moved by inertia, not by conviction. The extensive, almost three-hour race not only destroyed his physical endurance, fatigue also clouded his mind. Dizzy he ran in the opposite direction when he reached the White City track. Moved by that spirit, the judges left for a moment their dry posture and got to redirect Pietri's erratic steps with shouts and shoves. The athlete was 100 meters away from the finishing line, but fell once, twice, thrice. The last crash seemed definitive: there were no forces to recover the vertical. The American John Hayes entered the stadium and the crowd exploded to try to revive the Italian. People did not want to see the bars and stars flag waving champion again, and screamed uncontrollably to try to wake up Pietri. But the little pastry chef with thick and dark moustaches did not respond. With the sports protocol surpassed by the sour anti-Yankee rejection, one of the referees and people from the public passed from the grass to the ashes to help the Italian. They stood him up and pushed him to glory. Stuttering, Dorando cut the tape 30 seconds before Hayes, whose walk was not precisely overwhelming.

The awards ceremony advanced with a tricolor emblem flaming proudly for his son: red, white…and green. Blue was over. A few meters from the proud flagstaff, US team leaders demanded that Pietri must be disqualified. They rightly argued that the champion received illegal aid. The referees knew that they must take a fair but unpopular decision, and they extended the declaration so that the stands could release as many spectators as possible. Pietri was stripped of his title, but his misfortune only managed to multiply his popularity. *The Daily Mail* launched a collection and raised 300 pounds for the tiny corridor that arrived from the Emilia-Romagna. Moved, Queen Alejandra honourued him with a golden cup. The composer Irving Berlin, excited by the feat, dedicated a song to him. The honeys of success impelled Pietri to pursue another career as a professional runner. Almost unbeatable, he won seventeen out of twenty-two races. One of them is memorable: on 25 November 1908, at the Madison Square Garden he took revenge on Hayes in a 'face-to-face' duel. Its reputation arrived even to the distant Buenos Aires, where, on 24 May 1910, he conquered the centennial marathon.

LONELY RUNNER

Rarely an Olympic race had a final as disconcerting as the 400-meter event, held on 25 July at the White City Stadium: the competition was completed with only one runner. Of course, this unusual situation has a justification. After two qualifying rounds, four athletes were classified to fight for gold on 24 July : Americans John Taylor, John Carpenter and Williams Robbins, and Englishman, Wyndham Halswelle, naturally the spectators' favourite. After the starting shot, the sprinters came out in a compact group and upon reaching the final stretch, Carpenter took a lead by a hair and won the competition in front of the English, in 48.4 seconds.

However, Halswelle complained about an alleged intentional elbow in the chest received from the winner, which blocked him to catch the line in the first place. Judges Roscoe Badger and David Basan, both British, agreed that the protest was legitimate and decided to invalidate the race, order its repetition the next day and without the presence of Carpenter, who was disqualified for unsportsmanlike conduct. The American team rejected the ruling and claimed that Carpenter's victory be ratified. The visiting managers assured that, if there had been a hit, it had been absolutely fortuitous. As the judges stood firm and their decision was supported by the organisers, the American team decided to withdraw Robbins and Taylor and not go to White City to intervene in the new final. Who did appear was Halswelle to participate in a grotesque situation: instead of being directly anointed winner, the officers forced him to run again...against anyone. The English accepted to participate in the farce and crossed the 400 meters in 50 seconds to receive a gold medal that was already his anyway. In addition, there was no silver or bronze for any other athlete. The controversial decision also extinguished the sporting flame of Halswelle: convinced of having been used in the eternal dispute between Yankees and the British, the runner left athletics and only returned to the tracks in Scotland, the land of their ancestors.

On 31 March 1915, during the First World War, while one column of the British army was advancing from the French city of Laventie to the border with Belgium, the moustached face of Captain Wyndham Halswelle was shattered by the accurate projectile of a German sniper. Almost ninety years later, the name of the lone runner entered the Edinburgh Scottish Sport, Hall of Fame.

IN THE RULE OF THE FATHER

The boxing championship developed at the Northampton Institute had several peculiarities. The first, that all the fighting took place on the same day, 27 October, in a marathon day. The second, that the medal display table was monopolised by British fighters. The podiums of four of the five categories—bantam, feather, light, middle and superheavy weight—were made up of local representatives. The exception was in 'mediums,' whose final was qualified by Australian Reginald 'Snowy' Baker, a versatile athlete who in London also competed in diving and swimming. Snowy (nicknamed after his prematurely white hair at the age of twenty-four) won his first three fights and, in the final match, faced John Douglas, a strong guy who threw him on the canvas in the second round. However, Baker recovered and matched the contest based on a good defense and precise punches. The fight ended with the two contestants standing, so it was necessary to appeal to the decision of the referee. Hearing that the adverse verdict, Snowy began a strong protest and even had to be contained by other fighters and some assistants so that he could not attack the referee. When he calmed down a bit, Baker withdrew from the stage without accepting the prize, what he believed unfair. Why did he consider it unfair? Because the referee John Douglas not only had the same name as the Golden champ: he was also his father.

STOCKHOLM 1912

Those who had the opportunity to witness the Games before the First World War said that the Stockholm 1912 Olympiad was very close to perfection. The credit goes to a gratifying combination of factors, among which stood out a neat organisation without problems over three weeks: the debut of the electric stopwatch and the 'photo-finish', the first participation of athletes of the five continents, a great investment in infrastructure and excellent climatic conditions, favoured by the extensive sunny days of that part of the planet so close to the North Pole. The Swedish experience only had a cloud, unfortunately rather dark: the disqualification of the American aboriginal Jim Thorpe for having played baseball as a professional a few months ago—'amateurism' returned with its punches of eliticism.

Sweden, with 65 medals (24 golds), was placed at the top of the ranking of countries after taking advantage of its local status. Much of that glory was due to the surname Carlberg: the twins Gustaf Vilhelm Carlberg and Gustaf Carl Carlberg won 5 golds and 4 silvers in the various shooting events. The United States finished second in the general count, but returned home with more golds than the organising nation: 26.

Boxing was not included in this edition because this discipline was prohibited by law in Sweden back those days, but as a counterpart, the women could enjoy their first female swimming contests.

THE PROFESSIONAL

The American athletic team arrived at Stockholm with a stellar figure: Oklahoma's giant Jim Thorpe. Son of an Irishman and an aboriginal pottawatomie, this remarkable twenty-three-year-old athlete—who was also known by his native name 'Wa-tho-huk', 'Shining Path' in English—had exceptional conditions that allowed him to stand out in the most diverse disciplines. On 7 July, in the pentathlon—an event abolished after the Games of Paris 1924—Thorpe completed with great skill the tests of long jump, discus and javelin throw, 200 and 1500 meters, and won by more than 300 points (according to the system of current rating) against the Norwegian national Ferdinand Bie, who won the silver medal. Some historians say that the champion finished improving his technique at sea, aboard the ship S.S. Finland that moved the North American delegation. A week later, in the decathlon that lasted between 13–15 July, the big man got notable records at 100, 400 and 1500 meters, long and high jump, shot-put, disc and javelin throw, pole vault and 110-meter hurdles. Thorpe won gold with an even greater difference: more than 600 points over Sweden's Hugo Wieslander, second in the general table. The skill of the American moved the Swedish king Gustaf V, who unconcerned with the protocol, left the official box and approached the athlete to shake his hand and tell him that 'You, sir, are the greatest athlete in the world'. Shy and somewhat uncomfortable about the situation, Thorpe could barely sketch a smile and answer 'Thank you, King'. It is assured that the monarch also intended to have a private interview with the champion but the American preferred to participate in a new event: to drink beer in a tavern. It seems that Thorpe got another record that afternoon.

In 1913, at the request of a complaint, the IOC initiated an investigation to determine if Thorpe had violated the strict rules of amateurism. The analysis determined that effectively between 1909 and

1910 the athlete had intervened two seasons in the Eastern Carolina League of baseball with a Rocky Mount team, which had paid him 2 USD per game. Amateur Athletic Union secretary, James Edward Sullivan, took the case very severely and ruled against Thorpe, although he excused himself for what he considered the behaviour of 'an aboriginal student' who 'didn't know' what he was doing. He also claimed that he had at least the courage to act with his own name and not with a fake one, as other players had done. Thorpe lost his Olympic titles and was forced to return his medals. Since the IOC had given him the 'professional' status, the big guy agreed to join the Major League New York Giants baseball team. After playing in two other clubs—Cincinnati Reds and Boston Braves—Thorpe changed sport and joined the Ohio Canton Bulldogs of the American football league. He also wore the shirt of other squads such as Cleveland Indiana, Oorang Indians and Chicago Cardinals. Retired from the sport, 'Shining Path' acted in films and television programs, and in 1950 he was distinguished as 'the best American football player' and 'the best male athlete' by the Associated Press. In January 1983, the IOC modified its position and agreed to revalidate the giant's titles, incorporate his name and his marks into official statistics and return his gold medals. Unfortunately, Thorpe had been dead for three decades. His children were excited about the badges that the athlete claimed, without luck, till the day of his death.

AUSTRALIAN FAIR PLAY

'I'm sorry, guys, but you are eliminated for being late.' The American swimmers could neither believe nor did they want to what the judges told them on the morning of 7 July. They had arrived at Djurgårdsbrunnsviken at 9 am, the time they had been called to participate in the quarter-finals of the 100-meter freestyle. However, the organisers, in very good ways, explained to them that the contests had been carried out by 8 pm last night, which had been communicated 'in a timely manner' to one of the US sport officers.

The Hawaiian Duke Kahanamoku, one of the favourites, was disconsolate: he had practically toured the world to arrive in Stockholm and had trained on board the ship that took him to Europe in a small canvas pool tied to a rope to stay in the place. All in vain. The Olympic dream was diluted. When the discussion began to rise, Australian Cecil Healy, who had already run and passed to the semi-finals, came out in defense of American swimmers and assured the judges that if they did not allow Kahanamoku to intervene, he would resign in solidarity with the islander. The Australian's words moved the referees, who reviewed their position and authorised the Yankee's participation. On 10 July, Kahanamoku and Healy faced each other in the final. The Hawaiian, in a brilliant performance, got gold in 1:3.4, a second and two tenths faster than the Australian. Upon leaving the pool, Healy not only received the silver medal: he also won the congratulations of all Americans, especially Kahanamoku. This gesture lightened his bad taste of defeat. However, there was a rematch for the gentle Cecil: on 15 July, the 'Australasia' team, made up of three Australians—Healy, Les Boardman and Harold Hardwick—and a New Zealander, Malcolm Champion, took possession of the gold in the 4x200 post freestyle and relegated the American quartet to the second place.

MARATHON OF DEATH

The traditional marathon on Sunday, 14 July, was developed amidst overwhelming heat—the chronicles of the time assure that the mercury of the thermometers exceeded 30°C and there was a blazing sun. It was so devastating that the Portuguese Francisco Lázaro, who led the marathon at 29 kilometer, fell and almost collapsed when he tried to climb a hill in the town of Öfver-Järv. Lázaro, a twenty-one-year-old winner of the Lisbon marathon, was rushed to the Seraphim hospital, where he died the following morning. Armando Cortesão, a Portuguese athlete, who in Stockholm competed in the 400 and 800 meters, considered that the death of his compatriot had two causes: the first, to cover his body with fat, supposedly to protect himself from the sun—'We found him smearing shortly before departure and we tried to take a shower, but there was no time. He ran covered with sebum, which covered his skin pores and prevented him from perspiring,' he recalled. The second reason was that Lazarus competed 'with his head uncovered', without even a cap to shield it from the scorching sun. The body of the unfortunate athlete was repatriated two months later, thanks to the fact that one of his colleagues organised a collection in order to raise the money needed for the final trip.

THE LONGEST RACE IN HISTORY

After the marathon, the Japanese delegation denounced the disappearance of its only competitor: Shizo Kanakuri. The twenty-year-old Japanese athlete's trail had evaporated in the middle of the arduous race. The organisers and numerous policemen tried in vain to find the eastern corridor around the circuit: nobody had seen him, nobody knew anything about him. Evicted, the Japanese group had to return to its country with one less man. Fifty years later, a Swedish journalist who had traveled to Japan and casually passed through Tamana, the hometown of Kanakuri, decided to make a stop to try to find out what the end of the mysterious story had been. After consulting some neighbours, the chronicler discovered the former athlete sitting in a bar. Surprised by the presence of the Swede, Kanakuri agreed to tell his story: shortly before reaching 30 kilometer, in the town of Tureberg, he felt bad, sunburned because of the strong sunrays. The Japanese was invited by a spectator to enter to his house to rest and drink something.

After enjoying several fruit juices, the runner fell asleep. Hours later, upon waking up, Kanakuri felt ashamed and did not want to meet again with his companions and embarked on his own a very long journey back home, through Russia. After the First World War, the marathoner returned to represent his country in the Games: he came in 16th place in Antwerp 1920 and left again in Paris 1924, something that had not been published in the Swedish newspapers. The journalist presented the story of the Japanese athlete, and a few years later, in 1967, a Stockholm television channel invited Kanakuri to end his Swedish career. Seventy-six-year-old, the old man completed step by step the 42,195-meter route from the point he had left. Kanakuri arrived at the 'finishing line' 54 years, 8 months, 6 days, 8 hours, 32 minutes and 20 seconds later, recording thelongest marathon run in the history.

GOLDEN TRICK

Among so many adventures, the Stockholm marathon was won by the South African policeman Kennedy McArthur. Second, a minute later, another South African racer, Christian Gitsham, arrived enraged. Far from celebrating the double of his country with McArthur, Gitsham tried to attack the policeman, whom he accused of having had an attitude far from fair play. According to his story, the two South Africans, after seizing the top of the competition, thanks to the tragic abandonment of the Portuguese Francisco Lázaro, had agreed to stop together to drink water. A few miles from the stadium, noticing that they had a significant advantage, Gitsham proposed McArthur to make a pause. The police, according to the version of the second, slowed down, but as soon as Gitsham began to drink with content, he resumed the race at full speed. Moments later, upon discovering that he had been deceived, Gitsham returned to the race, desperate to reach his countryman, but by then he had already achieved enough advantage to be crowned with the olive leaves. The silver medalist remained angry for eight years, and when the Games returned after the war, he traveled to Antwerp for the rematch. There, Gitsham again dominated the contest but, just five kilometers from the finishing line, a shoe was broken, his foot was injured and he had to withdraw, disconsolate. It is said that meanwhile, in South Africa, a policeman raised his glass to toast for the triumph of the Finnish, Hannes Kolehmainen.

EXPENSIVE FALL

The result of the football tournament was interesting because the podium of the previous edition was repeated. Great Britain defeated Denmark for gold—in this case, after winning 4–2 on 4 July at the Olympic stadium—and Holland also won the bronze. The championship had more registrants, nine, though all European, and while the semi-finals and finals were developing, the organisers devised a 'consolation' tournament for the eliminated teams. In one of those matches, Germany humiliated Russia with a result 16–0, with 10 goals from striker Gottfried Fuchs, who thus equalled the record of Denmark's Sophus Nielsen of 1908, an Olympic mark still unbeaten. The resounding fall had repercussions on the other side of the Baltic Sea: Nicholas II (the last czar of Russia, deposed by the 1917 revolution and murdered a year later), angry at what he considered a shameful result for his homeland, refused to pay the trip back to players and managers. The athletes and their representatives accepted the punishment in silence and paid the train back to Moscow from their pocket. No one protested. Everyone knew that if they opened their mouth, the next stop of the trip would be Siberia.

ANTWERP 1920

According to the IOC, Antwerp 1920 was not the sixth game, but the seventh. 'An Olympic Game may not be held, but its figure remains,' said Pierre de Coubertin, and decreed that, for the record, the sixth edition reserved for Berlin was computed as such, although the only 'sport' that was played in Europe that year was to kill people in the trenches of the First World War. The same would happen later with the Games of 1940 and 1944, awarded to Tokyo and London, respectively. Why, at the end of the fighting, the German capital was not reappointed for 1920? Because the IOC member countries blamed the German nation for the terrible conflict, which left about ten million dead. In addition to eliminating the host status of Berlin, Germany was not invited to participate in Antwerp. The Belgians did not really want to welcome the same people who had caused so much violence and destruction. With the consent of Coubertin (who at the age of fifty came to act in the war as a volunteer, although he did not serve in the front but collaborated from a position in the rearguard), there were also no calls to other states of the defeated side: Austria, Hungary (both member nations of the dismembered Austro-Hungarian Empire), Bulgaria and Turkey (head of the Turkish-Ottoman Empire). Russia, though acted in the winning group, resigned to intervene for being submerged in a bloody civil war that faced the Tsarists—reinforced with troops from other countries in Europe and Asia—with the powerful Bolshevik Red Army, which was imposed in 1923. This immense state would just return to the Games in 1952, although as the Union of Soviet Socialist Republics (USSR).

Two years after the peace was recovered, the fields of Belgium continued to be furrowed by trenches and barbed wires. As happened many times in history, the Franco–Dutch nation served as a battlefield to settle the rivalries of the old continent. When the detonations of the cannons ceased and the smoke from the gunpowder dissipated, the IOC decided to create a symbol as a synonym for world peace: the Olympic flag with five interlocking rings—blue, yellow, green, black and red—on a white background, which represent the colours of all the pavilions of the world. It is said that these five rings also symbolise one continent each—the blue one, Oceania; the yellow, Asia; the green, Europe; the black, Africa; the red, America—but this interpretation was not officially accepted by the IOC. Also in this Game the 'Olympic Oath' was incorporated, which is read in each edition by an athlete representing all the participants involved. The original text stated: 'We swear that we will take part in the Olympic Games in a spirit of chivalry, for the honour of our country and for the glory of sport'. Currently, this sentence has undergone slight modifications, such as replacing 'swearing' with 'promising', and expressing against the use of stimulants: 'On behalf of all competitors, I promise that we will participate in these Olympic Games, respecting and following the rules that govern them, committing ourselves to a sport without doping and without drugs, with the true spirit of sportsmanship, for the glory of the sport and the honour of our teams'.

Interestingly, swimming competitions developed in the pits of ancient castles of the city. Ice hockey and figure skating were included although both disciplines would be passed to the Winter Games four years later. The winners' medals were not made of gold, but of vermeil, a kind of golden silver of much less value. The host country was not in a position to waste its resources, so necessary to renovate buildings destroyed by the war. However, the Olympic stadium was built in the Beerschot neighborhood, with a capacity for 40,000 spectators. It was only full of spectators for the final of the football tournament.

For the sports chronicle, the United States won the most medals (94, of which 41 golds), partly thanks to the aim of Willis Augustus Lee, a Kentucky shooter who won 6 golds, 1 silver and 1 bronze in different categories. After the previous marathonic editions (with the exception of Athens, which only lasted one week), the Antwerp Games expanded over fifteen days, a format that satisfied both organisers and athletes and was sealed forever.

CHAMPION MOM

The Swedish Magda Julin left the spectators open-mouthed who approached the Palais de Glace d'Anvers to enjoy the women's ice skating championship on 25 April . First, for her exquisite performance which earned the gold medal; second, because she was four months pregnant. Julin was the only woman in Olympic history to obtain a gold—but not the only one to intervene in the Games—with a tot inside. In fact, the German Cornelia Pfohl did not participate pregnant in only Olympiad, but in two: in Sydney 2000 she won the bronze medal gestating her first daughter, and in Athens 2004, of her second child. Cornelia acted in the archery contest, a sport that did not put her condition at risk. In the Greek capital, the German was pregnant for thirty weeks, and said goodbye without entering the podium. 'I decided to compete because I felt very good and the doctors had guaranteed me that there would be no problems. I would never have accepted if they told me there were risks,' proclaimed the archer.

Another interesting case was protagonised by the American Juno Stover-Irwin, who intervened in the contest of diving in Helsinki 1952 with a gravity of almost four months. Her condition was not a problem to obtain a bronze medal. Four years later, in Melbourne, the American deployed a more daring routine and took the silver medal.

LENT GOLD

The first official delegation sent by Brazil to the Olympic Games participated in the 1920 Antwerp edition. The representation consisted of twenty-one competitors, all men, who traveled to participate in swimming, water polo, rowing, diving and shooting tournaments. The group left Rio de Janeiro aboard the Curvello steamboat, with third-class passages and forced to occupy very uncomfortable cabins. To get to Europe well rested, the athletes decided to sleep in the first class dining room: they lay on the floor when dinner was over and got up before the breakfast service began. In the middle of the crossing, the athletes learned that their ship planned to arrive in Antwerp at an inconvenient date, several days after the start of the sport event and with most of the competitions already over. Therefore, they went down in the port of Lisbon and continued by rail, changing trains in Spain and France. Some historians say that, when they finally arrived in Antwerp, after twenty-seven days of extensive travel, the Brazilian Army Lieutenant Guilherme Paraense discovered that he had lost the suitcase in which he carried his armament. Another version asserts that, already installed in the polygon of competition in the town of Bewerloo, the South Americans became friends with their American colleagues, who were sorry to discover the painful state of the Verdeamarelo arsenal. In any case, the Americans lent two Colt guns and 2000 bullets to their Brazilian rivals. Thanks to the generous contribution, Paraense won the gold medal in the 'rapid-fire pistol' category with just 2 points ahead of the American Raymond Bracken, 274–272. The Yankee team captain, Colonel George Sanders, almost fainted!

In the 'free pistol' category, Sanders was very close to a heart attack: Karl Frederick (fourth in the previous contest) beat Brazil's Afrânio da Costa by a hair in the gold medal dispute. In the team tournament, Brazil won its third medal, in this case bronze, in the category 'military revolver teams' from 50 meters (Sebastião Wolf, Dario Barbosa and Fernando Soledade competed together with Paraense and da Costa), behind the Americans (gold) and the Swedish (silver). The Brazilian delegation returned home with three medals—the performances in the other Olympic contests were very weak—and the joy of having made the right decision to get off at Curvello in Lisbon. If they had completed the trip to Antwerp on the ship, the harvest would have been reduced to zero since the shooting competition was one of the first ones on the calendar.

FINNS

Since the resurgence of the Games, the track and field athletic events had, as exclusive winners, the US representatives. Until the Antwerp edition, no team could shade the Yankee squad in races, jumps and throws. However, in the sixth Olympiad, a small country in northern Europe achieved a feat that seemed impossible: to match the United States in terms of gold. Thanks to the magnificent performance of Paavo Nurmi, who won three competitions, Finland added 9 gold medals, the same amount as the powerful American delegation(although it won 12 silvers and 8 bronzes, against 4 and 3, respectively, of the Nordic squad). Nurmi prevailed in the 10,000meters and cross-country in two categories—individual and by teams—and obtained the silver in 5000 meters. This great runner would then add another five golds in Paris

1924 and a ninth in Amsterdam 1928. Another notable contribution came from the feet of Johan 'Hannes' Kolehmainen, a Stockholm hero with 3 golds and 1 silver, who won the marathon. Kolehmainen, who lived in New York, agreed to compete in Belgium because his country's Olympic committee paid him the ticket to Antwerp. At thirty-one years of age, Hannes enrolled in the marathon because he considered that, at his age, he was not in a position to participate in the 5000, 10,000 meters and individual cross-country, the three competitions he had won eight years back in Stockholm.

THE BIG SURPRISE

Possibly the most amazing athletic victory of these Games was provided by the American Allen Woodring, a student at the University of Syracuse, in the 200 meters. Woodring, who had not qualified to represent his country in the preliminaries back in the United States, arrived in Antwerp, thanks to the injury of the fourth selected, George Massengale. The boy managed to pass the first two qualifiers on 19 August, and the next morning, won the second semi-final, even though his worn shoes opened in the final sprint. Woodring did not have a spare pair, so he had to borrow one. However, the footwear he got was not suitable because the nails were too long, almost double that of his. Anxious of falling on the track, the young man tried to file the grips, but did not have enough time or the necessary tools. Lost in every quarter, Woodring went in search of the miracle and the miracle arrived: a strong and passing downpour drenched the Olympic stadium and softened its ash track too much. For that unexpected surface, the longer nails offered the perfect grip. Woodring, the student who had not qualified for the Games, the great American surprise, had his best race in life and returned home proudly with a gold medal around his neck.

DRINK AND DIET

'Take this and you will be invincible,' the French coach told Joseph Guillemot. Although he trusted his boy, the trainer did not know how he would respond to the demanding 5000 meters, especially after having breathed toxic gases in the Great War, fighting against the Germans. Some doctors had even considered that the exposure to poisonous vapours had ruined Guillemot's lungs. The runner drank the mysterious concoction and on 17 August he jumped onto the track of Beerschot Stadium to face fourteen opponents, including the Finnish Paavo Nurmi, a great favourite. Just two laps after the start, the French and the Finn took the lead of the race and increased their advantage with each turn. The head-to-head dispute was vibrant until just 200 meters from the finishing line, where Guillemot took off with a bright sprint and won the gold medal. After hugging his coach, the happy winner wanted to know what the mysterious and miraculous potion contained. The coach smiled for a moment, to put a quota of suspense to his response, and replied that it was only a mixture of rum, water and egg yolks.

On 20 August, the 10,000-meter final, where once again Guillemot and Nurmi faced each other, was scheduled for 5:30 pm. However, at the request of King Albert I of Belgium, who wished to witness the duel but also attend an art exhibition that afternoon, the organisers advanced the race three hours. The Frenchman, who had enjoyed a Pantagruleic lunch, protested the decision and demanded that the original schedule be maintained. Given the refusal of the judges, he had no choice but to go out on the track with a full stomach. Likewise, he had to wear borrowed shoes, two larger numbers, because his had been stolen in the locker room. As in the previous contest, Nurmi and Guillemot led the squad with slack. This time, however, the one who dominated the final sprint was the Finn, who finished the competition at 31:45.8, just a second and a half ahead of the Frenchman. Guillemot approached to greet the winner, but a second before shaking his hand he vomited all his lunch on Nurmi's shoes. The Finn did not stop smiling despite the unpleasant incident. The Frenchman wanted to know why his winner had not suffered stomach cramps, like him. Nurmi explained that he had also been surprised by the advancement of the race, but he had not been affected by any indisposition because he had the habit of following a very frugal diet based on fish and whole wheat bread. With this victory, the remarkable Finnish runner began a golden Olympic career that accumulated nine golds in three Games.

FROZEN RESULT

The match was even. Spain and Italy did not take advantage and tied in a goal in the first game of the water polo tournament, which was held on 22 August in the Stade Nautique pool. At the end of the stipulated time, with a balanced scoreboard, the judges announced that there would be an extra time to define the winner. But, to the surprise of the public, the organisers, the referees and even the Iberians, the Italian boys left the pool and announced that they were retiring. 'We don't want to spend another minute in the water. It's freezing!', they justified themselves. The warm Olympic spirit of the 'azzurri' allowed the Spaniards to continue in the competition, although for a short time: in the following clash they fell 9–0 against the United Kingdom (who would later win the gold medal against the local team) and 5–0 to the United States.

THE TWO SEASONS

When he arrived in Belgium, Yankee Edward 'Eddie' Eagan had two boxing titles on his shoulders: one as champion of the American Athletic Union (AAU) and another as British monarch, thanks to his Irish blood. On 24 August, Eagan added a new award to his career by defeating the Norwegian Sverre Sørsdal in the light-heavyweight final, played at La Salle des Fêtes de la Zoologie. In the next Olympic edition, held in Paris, the young man born in Denver, Colorado, sought to add more laurels to his career in the greater of the categories, but his aspirations quickly fell apart when he brutally collided with the fists of British Arthur Clifton, who knocked him out in the first round. The brutal beating announced the end of his pugilistic career. However, that limit did not extend to other disciplines. In 1932, the former boxer was invited to join a four-man bobsled team that was preparing for the Winter Games that would be held in Lake Placid, a small town located in the Adirondack Mountains, in the state of New York. Eagan accepted, and with just a few training landslides, adapted perfectly to the quartet that was awarded gold in the sled specialty. With this victory, the former fighter not only removed the bad Parisian taste, but also became the only athlete to win the Olympic gold at the Summer and Winter Games.

THE COMMONER

American construction worker John Brendan Kelly was one of the best rowers of his time. In Antwerp, he got a great double success: he won gold in the single and double sculls (in the second case, alongside Paul Costello) with just half an hour's difference. Kelly thus had his revenge for the disappointment of not being accepted in a select race in London, a few weeks before. The reason? He was a simple commoner in charge of manual labour. On 29 August, just after the second race, the American left his boat on the Willebroek channel, approached the British team and handed them his green beanie to be sent to King George V of England. But before that, with a pen he wrote on the visor an ironic dedication: 'Greetings from a bricklayer'. Over the years, Kelly not only became one of the richest men in Philadelphia, whose company would build numerous churches and schools in that city of the state of Pennsylvania, but was closely linked to the European nobility when his daughter, Grace Kelly, married Prince Raniero of Monaco on 19 April 1956.

THE SOUVENIR

For Haig 'Hal' Prieste, to return home with just a bronze medal obtained in a diving contest seemed too little. Much more, seeing how two golds gleamed in the chest of his friend Duke Kahanamoku. 'Take that away,' the Hawaiian swimmer spurred him. Prieste looked at the mast and his eyes shone. He had liked the idea. With great agility, he climbed the white-painted wood and, with an accurate swipe, seized the fabric. The Olympic flag, the brand new emblem with the five intertwined rings, was presented by the IOC in Antwerp. The next day, the robbery surprised the local organisers, who were offended by what they considered a crime against their ego. The victims requested police assistance to recover the standard, but the agents' effort was in vain: the banner did not appear anywhere. After overcoming customs controls, Prieste smiled from the deck of the Princess Mastroika on the move back home. He had not only achieved his souvenir but at the same time, humiliated the stand-offish Belgians. The most wanted treasure rested inside his suitcase as his exclusive trophy. In 1997, during a meeting of the American Olympic Committee, Prieste, visibly regretful for his mischief, offered the IOC president, the Spaniard Juan Antonio Samaranch, to return his loot. 'You can't be selfish with these things,' he told to the Olympic leader. Moved by the gesture, Samaranch invited Prieste to witness the 2000 Sydney Games and restore the flag in a special ceremony. At 103, the jumper traveled to Australia, again with the standard in his suitcase. For his attitude, the old man also received a gold medal. The historic emblem was taken to the IOC headquarters in Lausanne, Switzerland, where it was incorporated into the Olympic Museum. Prieste died on 18 April 2001, at the age of 104. His conscience was calm.

PARIS 1924

The eighth edition of the Games could well be entitled 'the rematch of Pierre de Coubertin'. About the end of his term as head of the IOC, the Frenchman took advantage of his political contacts to anoint his birthplace as host of a proper competition to erase, or at least liquefy, the lousy image left by the 1900 Games. This time, with the support of the Gallic government and with enough funds, Paris was truly the 'City of Lights' of sport. The Games had the great stage in the neighbuorhood of Colombes, northwest of the capital, where the magnificent Yves-du-Manoir stadium was built.

Without the participation of Germany—the French refused to receive their neighbours after the fateful First World War—the United States easily won the firt place at the medal table, with 99 pieces, 45 of them golden. However, the top stars of these Olympics were the Finns, headed by Paavo Nurmi (5 golds) and Ville Ritola (4 golds and 2 silvers), who practically monopolised the track and field athletic events.

One of the innovations of this edition was the Olympic Village. Although the idea of bringing together all the athletes in a single special estate would be formalised in 1932, a group of barracks located near the Colombes Stadium was used to accommodate several foreign delegations arriving in Paris.

HOUSES OF FIRE

The brand new Olympic Village started with the left foot: the first night there was a fire that devoured a dozen of small houses. The firemen, struggling to carry water and fight against the flames, desperately needed the helping hands of the athletes. The fire not only destroyed some small houses: it also took the life of a French fireman. To alleviate this misfortune, American athletes organised a collection for the widow and his children who raised 200 USD, a good sum of money at the time. This gesture was much appreciated by the Parisians, to the point that they loudly supported every performance of the Yankees.

BETWEEN GLASSES

The English sprinter Harold Abrahams did not like training much. Instead of practising, he preferred to spend long hours drinking beer and smoking cigars. Seeing him enjoy the 'dolce vita', the American athletes commented that this explained the poor performance of the British at the Games in Antwerp, where he did not qualify for the finals of the 100 and 200 meters, and was fourth in the 4x100 meters relay with his national team. However, in Paris, Abrahams had a completely different performance. Not only did he qualify for the final 100 meters—along with four Americans and a New Zealander—but on 7 July, he seized the gold medal with full authority. The defeated Olympic monarch Charles 'Charlie' Paddock did not understand how he had fallen from first place in Antwerp to a humiliating fifth in the French capital, despite his strict and constant preparation. Paddock proposed to his compatriot Jackson Scholz, who had come second in the hectometer, to drink some beer the night before the end of the 200 meters, to see if the 'Abrahams method' worked for them to beat the English. On 9 July, well rested due to the relaxing foamy pints, Scholz and Paddock exploded on the track and got gold and silver, respectively. The proverb 'he who lives by the sword, dies by the sword' fits Abrahams perfectly, who reached the finishing line in sixth place.

GHOST

The athletic contests developed in the middle of an unusual heat that turned the City of Light into an oven. The high temperatures, which according to the newspapers of the time, exceeded 40°C, caused several competitors sheer discomfort. On 12 July, during the performance of the cross-country race (individual and team, at the same time), British Arthur Sewell entered the stadium of Colombes staggering. Stunned by the strain and dehydration, he crashed into a wall, opened his head and fell faint with his face covered with blood. Another athlete who broke down was the Spaniard José Andía, who vanished and had to be admitted to a hospital, where he remained hospitalised for several days. In this context, the extraordinary performance of the Finns Viljo 'Ville' Ritola and Paavo Nurmi surprised the spectators and the organisers of the event. Ritola added four gold medals (10,000 meters, with a world record; 3000 meters steeplechase individual and team; and cross-country team) and two silver ones (5000 meters and individual cross-country). Nurmi, called 'the flying Finnish' or 'the ghost', turned everything he touched into gold: 1500 meters, 5000 meters, 3000 meters in teams, individual cross-country and teams, respectively. The coaches of the squad from Finland asked Nurmi not to act in the 10,000 meters—which he had won in Antwerp and would dominate in Amsterdam four years later—to keep fresh for the rest of the contests. Disapointed, the runner agreed though he considered himself in a position to add that demanding test to his calendar. The phantom seemed little affected by the powerful heat, to the point that he prevailed in the 1500 and 5000 meters the same day, and with just one hour to rest. In just three Games (Antwerp, Paris and Amsterdam) Nurmi added nine golds and three silvers.

FRACTURED LEG, STEEL HEART

'I'm sorry, but you can't run again.' The sentence of the traumatologist caused the Finnish Albin Stenroos more pain than the fracture of his leg itself. The career of the athlete, who in Stockholm 1912 had won bronze in the 10,000 meters and silver in cross-country teams, was finished at just thirty years of age. But sometimes the doctor proposes and the one who disposes is the patient. Steenroos, a young man of strong convictions, was not defeated by adversity. Once the bone welded, Stenroos gradually began to recover the mobility of his limb. First walking, then jogging, later running. He would not arrive in time for the Antwerp Games, but a light of hope illuminated Paris. After four years of enormous efforts, the athlete was ready to travel to the French capital. However, the only place the coaches offered him was in the marathon, along with other long-distance runners who had been left out of the team for the other contests. Stenroos accepted, although he had never run 42 kilometers: at age thirty-five he had already overcome too many adversities to surrender to a new obstacle. On 13 July, the Finn gave a masterclass of self-esteem by obtaining the gold medal with 6 minutes of advantage over the Italian Romeo Bertini, the second to reach the finishing line at the Colombes Stadium. Stenroos dominated the race from the start to the end with his leg recovered and an invincible heart, who knew nothing about medicine.

STIMULUS

American Lieutenant Sidney Hinds could not stand because of the sharp pain that pierced his right foot. The military was cursed for having agreed to intervene in that damn shooting contest in Reims. He had been convinced with the argument that the capital of the champagne was close to Paris and that tournament would serve to finish calibrating weapons very few days before the 1924 Games. Who had come up with such a ridiculous idea? To top it all, he had to share his duty with that undesirable Belgian, a rude man who began a bitter argument with the judges for no good reason. And then comes his carelessness. How could he leave his rifle loaded and uninsured, leaning against a table? The altercation generated shoves, the Belgian stumbled on the table, the gun fell, shot and his projectile made a target—the foot of the unfortunate Hinds. Only a couple of hours before the start of the '400-, 600- and 800-meter free rifle team' contest at the Camp de Châlons, the lieutenant could barely walk, much less stand firm to hold and fire his heavy rifle. Hinds left his room in the Games village limping and appeared in Earl's 'Tubby' Waller, the captain of the American squad. The team leader was completing the official form with the names of the competitors, among which was the lieutenant. 'I'm sorry, but I won't participate like that. I can't stand the pain anymore. Enroll another shooter in my place, please,' the wounded requested to Waller, who still did not look up from the paper. When the captain, famous for his strong character, finished writing, he stared at Hinds's eyes and, in a soft but firm tone, warned him: 'If you don't show up to compete, I myself am going to shoot you on the other foot'. Motivated by Waller's *warm* support, Hinds displayed the best performance of his life, and won the gold medal.

SCANDAL

The rugby tournament was, without doubt, the most anticipated event for the French. The local players and fans burned for revenge for the humiliating defeat in Antwerp against the United States. In France, where this sport enjoys a fervent popularity, the shameful fall against a country in which the game is practically non-existent could not be digested. For this edition, the Gauls armed one of the best national teams in their history and trained more than ever to wash their prestige stained with Belgian mud. Although only two rugby teams traveled to the Parisian Games, the United States and Romania, the local fans were not worried about the lean call. They only cared about the presence of the Yankees, eager to regain their lost honour. On Sunday, 4 May, the French dream was in motion, thanks to an overwhelming victory against Romania, by 61–3. A few days later, the US squad also surpassed the Romanian, although by a narrower score, 37–0. On Sunday 18 May, the party was ready at the Colombes Stadium. Bookmakers gave a 20–1 local advantage. The match was won before the initial whistle: the inexperienced Yankees had no chance against the local power. Even some of the visitors had just started playing rugby six months before. However, sometimes history repeats itself. Fifty thousand fans went from the bustling fervor to the muted disenchantment at the inevitable: another incredible defeat, in this case by 17–3. The Americans, less technical, showed unusual bravery. The meeting had passages of great violence, especially when the American Alan Valentine, a giant of 110 kilos, injured the great local star, the wing Adolphe Jaureguy. A few minutes before another embarrassing fall took place, the French fans first attacked a small group of visiting supporters, many of whom ended up in hospital. Then, the bellicose spectators jumped to the pitch to hit the American players, who had to take refuge in the locker room. The athletes were able to escape several hours later, in the middle of an iron police operation. The awards ceremony, of course, was suspended because of the scandal. When knowing the seriousness of the incidents, foreign teams refused to risk the integrity of their men in the face of the brutal vandalism of Parisian fans.

With the United States, French rugby had to wait fifty-two years to collect its rematch. Both squads met again on 12 June 1976 in a 'friendly' match held in the city of Chicago, where Europeans were finally able to prevail by 33–14.

TRIUMPH BROUGHT BY TOOTH

The boxing match that British Harry Mallin and Frenchman Roger Brousse starred in the Vélodrome d'Hiver was very even. So much so that the fight, corresponding to the middleweight category, was defined by a split decision, 2–1, in favour of the local fighter. However, before getting out of the ring, Mallin—who was defending the gold he had obtained in Antwerp—approached to the referee and showed him the teeth marks that his rival had left in his chest when he bit him in the last round. Upon checking the injury, the judges reversed their decision and disqualified the French boxer. Mallin went to the semi-finals and, two days later, repeated the gold medal against his countryman, John Elliott.

AMSTERDAM 1928

The Amsterdam Olympic was the great door to the modern Olympics: for the first time, female participation in athletic track and field events was allowed. This had a lot to do with the IOC leadership falling on the Belgian Henri de Baillet-Latour, who took the post of Pierre de Coubertin in 1925—although the French continued as 'Honourary President' until his death in 1937. There were only five events in which women competed—100 meters and 800 meters, 4x100 meters relay, high jump and disc throw—against twenty-two of the men, but this turn was a great advance towards the future of sport to eliminate the misogynist ideals of leaders like Coubertin. The American Elizabeth Robinson, only sixteen years old, had the privilege of receiving the first gold medal as a woman in the Athletic Olympic history when, on 31 July, she won the 100-meter race.

Within the institutional framework, it was decided that Greece, mother nation of the Games, had the honour of opening the parade of each Olympic edition. It was also determined that the host country would close the ceremony. The first Olympic flame was also included in the stadium, on the Marathon Tower designed by Dutch architect Jan Wils. For the torch that would carry the 'sacred' flames, we would have to wait until Berlin 1936, in which the torch race would be incorporated from the temple of Hera, in Olympia, to the main stadium. In Holland

and Los Angeles 1932, the Olympic fire was far from divine: it was lit with an ordinary lighter.

After the Olympic Village had been used for the first time in Paris in 1924, an exclusive space for competitors was not built in Amsterdam, since most of the delegations arrived in the Dutch capital by ships, which in addition to being a medium of transport, served as floating hotels. The Dutch did build a stadium for 40,000 spectators, which had two concentric tracks: inside, 400-meter long, the athletic one; on the outside, 500-meter cycling. Queen Wilhelmina van Oranje-Nassau refused to attend the stadium to witness the opening and closing ceremonies or the sports event, because she considered that the Olympics was 'a pagan festival'.

The United States was the country that won the most medals, with 56 (22 golds), followed by Germany, with 39—a great feat as they returned to the Games after two editions of suspension. Meanwhile, Italian gymnast Luigina Giavotti, only 11 years and 302 days old, became the youngest female Olympic medalist in history by winning silver as a member of her country's women's team.

THE SPRINTER WHO RETURNED FROM DEATH

The American teenager Elizabeth Robinson was so nervous that when she appeared on the track of the Olympic Stadium in Amsterdam for the 100-meter final race, on the morning of 31 July, she noticed blushing that she had worn two left foot slippers. The sixteen-year-old girl did not need warm-up exercises for the competition: the spectacle caused by the show and the race she had to do to change her right shoe were enough. 'Betty' was a few seconds after being eliminated because of her delay in recomposing her outfit, but at the moment of truth she left her anxiety at the starting line. When the opening shot of the contest was fired, the young woman exploded and in 12.2 seconds, a world record, she won the first gold medal as a woman athlete. In June 1931, while preparing to repeat gold in Los Angeles, Robinson was traveling aboard a plane that crashed near the city of Harvey, in the state of Illinois. Rescuers who found her among the twisted irons of the airplane thought she had died like most passengers. One of them placed her next to a corpse in the trunk of a car and took her directly to a funeral home. However, the sprinter's time had not come yet: an employee who was going to prepare Betty for her funeral discovered that the girl had not died, but she was in a coma. Robinson, who had suffered multiple fractures, including her hip and one leg, was admitted to a hospital, where she remained unconscious for seven months. Four years after the terrible incident, Robinson had not only overcome her injuries, but had returned to the tracks. In a preparatory tournament for the Games of Berlin 1936, the runner reached the record necessary to join the team that would compete in the 4x100 relay. On 9 August 1936, along with Helen Stephens (the new championin the 100 meters), Harriet Bland and Annette Rogers, the woman who returned from the death hung the gold medal around her neck.

BIG FOOT

Boasted by his bronze medal obtained in Paris in the 3000-meter team race, the American Joie Ray traveled at the age of thirty-four to the Dutch capital to participate in the 10,000 meters and in the marathon, two of the most tiresome contests. On 29 July, Ray had a very weak performance and finished in the fourteenth place, far from the winners. Six days later, the representative of the Illinois Athletic Club of Chicago ran like never before—42,195 meters—and for a very short time he ran out of a medal in the queen of competitions. Ray arrived at the stadium in the fifth place, just a minute behind the Finn Martti Marttelin, who won the bronze. Upon arriving at the locker room, the American could not take off his shoes. His feet had swollen enormously during the two and half hours the demanding competition lasted. Ray had to be assisted by a partner who, with a pair of scissors, managed to destroy the footwear and rescue the enlarged extremities. A basin with very cold water relieved the feet and the obvious anger of being so close to the podium.

FRENCH HELP

The elimination of the cross-country race from the athletic program denied the notable long-distance runner Paavo Nurmi from adding another gold medal to his voluminous harvest. Always hungry for laurels, the Finn decided to compete in the 3000-meter steeplechase, a contest in which he had never competed during an Olympiad, and had only run twice in his life. On 1 August, during the second qualifying race, Nurmi miscalculated the jump on the first wooden fence and fell on his back in the deepest part of the puddle. Upon seeing the accident, the French competitor Lucien Duquesne, who was running behind the Finn, stopped and helped him to stand up. Sore and with a slight twist in one foot, Nurmi returned to the race and remained shoulder to shoulder throughout the contest with his rescuer. Upon reaching the finishing line together and leading the way, Nurmi offered Duquesne to come first, but he, a great admirer of his rival, refused and crossed the line just a tenth behind his idol. In the final race, held on 4 August, the French had a poor performance and finished in the sixth place. Nurmi, who might not have qualified without Duquesne's assistance, stayed at the doors of his tenth gold.

NOT FIT FOR WOMEN

The leaders of the IOC exploded with fury. Henri Baillet-Latour, the new president of the entity, was stunned with the image of several participants of the 800-meter women's race lying on the ground, fainting, on the edge of the catastrophe. Nothing mattered to him that the German Lina Radke-Batschauer had won with a world record, followed by the Japanese Kinue Hitomi and the Swedish Inga Gentzel. For Baillet-Latour, the women's physique was not prepared to tolerate 'those efforts' and even he believed that running a distance greater than 200 meters represented not only a serious danger to their health, but also to their future motherhood. What the leader did not take into account was that the majority of the contestants of that competition held on 2 August were not properly trained girls and that many had registered without even prior experience. Anyway, fearful of a future eventuality, the Belgian manager removed from the women's Olympic calendar any pedestrian race exceeding 200 meters, a measure that remained until the Games of Rome 1960. More extensive contests such as 1500 meters appeared much later for women in the Olympics of Munich 1972 and the female marathon in Los Angeles 1984.

THE PERMISSION

Argentina had in Amsterdam the best boxing performance in history: two golds (Víctor Avendaño in light-heavyweight and Arturo Rodríguez in super heavyweight) and two silvers (Víctor Peralta in featherweight and Raúl Landini in welterweight). The great achievement not only had a sporting cause, but also a political one. It happened that Avendaño was doing the military service and his superiors, despite recognising his ability, had denied him permission to travel to Holland. One of the members of the Argentine Olympic committee, linked to the Executive Branch, requested a special authorisation from President Agustín Justo. The premier, who had sponsored the formation of an unusual delegation of 100 athletes, signed a decree to designate Avendaño as the athlete no. 101 of the group. The strong fighter traveled and won the first gold medal for his country at the individual level with the power of his fists.

SHE PUT HER CHEST TO ADVERSITY

The intense strokes of the German, Hildegard Schrader not only placed her at the head of the final race: the agitated movements also shattered one of the strapes of her swimsuit right in the middle of the contest, just in front of a very large audience that, on 9 August, had filled the swimming stadium of the Olympic Park to see the battle of 200 meters between the German and Marie Baron, the local contestant. With a bare breast, the beautiful Hildegard put aside all female modesty and concentrated on giving her maximum effort. Her determination and boldness were awarded with the gold medal. The male audience, meanwhile, forgot for a moment the national pride and applauded standing up the attractive Olympic spirit of the German, who relegated the Dutch to second place. Schrader won with a record of 3:12.6, a second and four tenths above the Olympic record she had recorded the day before, during the semi-final. 'If I had not suffered a fault in my clothing, I would have gone faster,' the blushing winner admitted. Which was this remarkable contest? Well, it seemed obvious: 200-meter breaststroke.

DUCK CROSSING

Australian carpenter Henry Pearce was an exceptional rower. With great expertise, despite his young age, Pearce had the best times in each qualifying test of the single sculls rowing category performed on the Sloten Channel, in the southwest of the city. On 10 August, during the final, the Australian made a notable difference with the second, the American Ken Myers. So wide was his advantage that shortly after reaching the final line, Pearce stopped to allow the crossing of a family of ducks. Despite his environment-friendly gesture, the Australian won the race easily. In addition to gold, Pearce's attitude should have received a Greenpeace medal.

LOS ANGELES 1932

After twenty-eight years and five consecutive European editions, the Games returned to the United States. The severe economic consequences of the Great Depression and the long distances to the 'far west' caused a sharp decline in terms of the number of participating countries (from forty-six to thirty-seven) and athletes (they were less than half that year in Amsterdam). In any case, despite the negative context, the IOC made a big effort—it provided monetary assistance for transportation and food—so that the ninth Olympiad was quite successful.

The local team showed a great superiority in the medal display table, with 44 gold, 36 silver and 30 bronze medals. The second-ranked country was Italy, which gathered 36 in total.

In this edition, the now traditional podium was used for the first time, to which the champion, the second and third of each sport go up to receive their prizes, contemplate the raising of their respective national flags and listen to the anthem of the winning country. The Olympic Village was also specially built, a series of fifty-five small houses where only male athletes were housed. The women were installed in the Chapman Park Hotel, a luxury hostel compared to the male lodge. Anyway, the organisers managed to make visitors feel at home. For this, for example, they got a foreign chef for each country to satisfy the competitors' tastes, and even installed a special post office identified as 'Olympic Village, California, USA'.

The football competition was not included for two reasons: first, it was believed that it would not arouse interest in the local spectators, better predisposed to other disciplines; second, there was a controversy between the IOC and the Fédération Internationale de Football Association (FIFA) over the growing influence of professionalism in this sport. However, both institutions, aware of the money generated from tickets, especially in Europe, solved the problem four years later— the ball rolled in Berlin.

FINNISH BOYCOTT

In April 1932, the International Federation of Amateur Athletics (IFAA), chaired by the Swedish businessman Sigfrid Edstrom, suspended runner Paavo Nurmi for the alleged violation of the rules of amateur sports. Edstrom accused the Finn of having collected cash during an athletic tour of the United States. Allegedly, a German sport executive presented evidence that the multi-champion of the Games had received money in four different cities to intervene in competitions. The controversial decision shocked the Olympic world: in Los Angeles, seventeen marathoners representing ten nations signed a petition to lift the suspension and allow Nurmi to compete, but the request did not prosper. The athlete, who had traveled 42,195 kilometers, was informed of the news of him being ruled out the day before the extensive race. In Finland, the Swedish leader Edstrom became the most hated person, to the point that the people of Helsinki refused to use the city trams because they had been manufactured by one of their companies. The protest was a symbol at the same time, because the great champion used to train by running behind the streetcars. However, years later, the IOC determined that the suspension had no grip and exonerated Nurmi. While he was already too old to intervene in the 1952 Games, the 'Flying Finnish' had the pleasure of being the torchbearer and lighting the Olympic flame in the Helsinki Olympic.

PROHIBITION

During the period of the Games, the liquor ban was in effect in the United States. This controversial measure called 'Prohibition' forbade the consumption, sale, production and importation of alcoholic beverages throughout the country. The fierce regulations caused awkward situations with delegations such as the French or Italian, who brought their own wines. When customs agents tried to seize the bottles, visiting athletes argued that the grape-based drink was essential for their diets. The athletes even threatened to boycott the competition. Finally, the US authorities had to allow the wine to enter and authorise its consumption into the Olympic Village. One of the outstanding drinkers of the French team was the disc thrower Jules Noël, who had, as luck, a ritual to drink a few glasses of champagne in the locker room before participating in the contest. In Los Angeles, Noël's best throw, which should ideally have placed him on the podium, was invalidated because the judge who had to supervise his performance had been distracted by looking at a pole vaulter. The Frenchman returned to throw his disc, but lost the bronze medal by 9 centimeters. Back in the dressing room, Noël strictly followed Napoléon Bonaparte's maxim on the champagne: 'We deserve it in victory, we need it in defeat.'

HUNGRY FOR GLORY

Swedish police officer Ivar Johansson easily won gold in the freestyle wrestling middleweight category. On 2 August, the twenty-nine-year-old Nordic beat Japanese Sumiyuki Kotani and Frenchman Emile Poilvé with ease; and the next day, in the final, he defeated Finnish Kyösti Aukusti Luukko with a little more effort. Not happy with a gold medal, Johansson enrolled in the Greco–Roman wrestling tournament. As his compatriot Axel Cadier was already registered for the contest for his weight, Ivar made a dangerous decision: he spent a day fasting and sweating in a sauna to qualify for the immediately lower category, welterweight. On an empty stomach and despite the wear generated by the other competition, Johansson beat the Hungarian Gyula Zombori. The next day, he got rid of Norwegian Arild Dahl and Estonian Osvald Käpp. On 7 August, the policeman, only fed with a fruit, defeated the Finnish Väinö Kajander to double his golden success.

FEMME FATALE

Although she had been living in the United States for nineteen years as 'Stella Walsh', Polish sprinter Stanislawa Walasiewicz represented her home country at the Los Angeles Games. The fast runner had an extraordinary performance in the 100 meters and surprised the spectators who filled the Coliseum Memorial when the gold was awarded with a new world record of 11.9 seconds. The Olympic history of 'Walsh' would not end there: in the next edition, Berlin 1936, he would get the silver medal in the hectometer, behind the young Helen Stephens. At the end of that feat, a Polish journalist accused the new Olympic champion of being a man. Stephens, without blushing, had no problem undressing in front of a group of judges to prove her femininity.

With two Olympic medals, Walsh returned to the United States, where she had an extensive career as a coach for new athletes. On 4 December 1980, while the former sprinter made a purchase in a small supermarket in the city of Cleveland, Ohio, a group of armed robbers broke into the scene. The owner of the establishment resisted the assault with a gun, which triggered a shooting. One of the bullets hit Walsh, who died immediately. When the body of the former athlete entered the morgue, the man in charge of the autopsy almost fainted: Stella was not Stella, but a man. The body, instead of female sexual organs, had a penis and two testicles. Despite the unusual find, Stanislawa Walasiewicz retains her Olympic title as a woman.

HONESTY

The comeback of the American Ralph Hill inflamed the crowd that filled the Los Angeles Coliseum on 5 August. From the last place in the 5000-meter race, Hill became 'shoulder to shoulder' with the leader of the competition, the Finnish Lauri Lehtinen. The deafening encouragement of the fans prompted the American to try a winning sprint, but he was twice blocked by Lehtinen, who ended up winning by just 30 centimeters. The spectators blew to the European a ferocious boo and a bunch of hard insults, which forced the presenter of the stadium, Bill Henry, to ask for silence. 'Ladies and gentlemen, please remember that these people are our guests,' said the announcer. Although he timidly acknowledged among his relatives that he had been the victim of a violation of the regulation, Hill preferred not to submit any claims. He told the judges that he hoped his rival had not crossed intentionally. 'What's wrong with winning a silver medal?', the runner asked a journalist from the *New York Times* who had tried to get a controversial statement from him. During the awards ceremony, Lehtinen invited the local athlete to share the first place on the podium, but the American preferred to stay on the second step. He was convinced that this was his rightful place. The Yankee nobility went around the world. In Sweden, where Finnish triumphs did not cause joy, the newspaper *Dagens Nyheter* called him 'the idol for boys who play sports in schools'—a description that made the honest Hill blush.

BARTENDER, ANOTHER ROUND

The judge in charge of controlling the laps of the Los Angeles Memorial Coliseum was very distracted. So much so that, due to his dismissal, the final of the 3000-meter steeplechase race, which took place on 6 August, was really 3460 meters. The controller counted the turns badly, forcing the athletes to give an extra lap. This affected the time of the winner, the Finn Volmari Iso-Hollo, who completed the race in 10:33.4. Five days earlier, in one of the qualifying events, Iso-Hollo had recorded 9:14.6, which was a new Olympic record. Anyway, the most affected was the American Joe McCluskey: when the official distance was completed, McCluskey had crossed the finishing line in second place. However, in the extra lap, he was overtaken by British Tom Evenson and was relegated to the bronze medal. The good of McCluskey—who was also the owner of the world record, with a time of 9:14.5—raised no complaints and settled for his third place. 'The race had only one finishing line', he said.

WINNING NUMBER

Argentina's Juan Carlos Zabala was one of the athletes who had signed the letter for the IOC to reverse the disqualification of Finnish Paavo Nurmi. This gesture was considered very commendable by the international press, since Zabala knew that his possibilities were not the same with the Finnish among the participants. When the measure against Nurmi was ratified, the Argentine had only one concern: the number that would correspond to him to act in the marathon, chosen by lottery. According to the newspaper *La Nación*, the runner 'ardently wished it was 12', the same one with which he had won in October previous year the traditional 'Peace Marathon' of the Slovak city of Košice. 'Great, then, was his joy when a delegate brought him the news that he had recieved the number 12. He strengthened his optimism and considered the fact as the good sign,' the newspaper said. On 7 August, Zabala, nicknamed 'El Ñandú Criollo', dominated the race from the beginning to the end and took over the gold medal with just 19 seconds ahead of British Sam Ferris. The Argentine just ran five marathons in his life, of which he only completed the two he won. Both, with the number '12' on his chest.

DEFLECTED SIGHT

The shooting range of the Los Angeles Police Department was the venue chosen for shooting competitions. On 12 August, the pistol contest was developed, and the next day the rifle test. On this second day, the Hungarian Antal Barát-Lemberkovits surprised the judges of the small-bore rifle event with one of his shots, which hit exactly the center of the bull's eye. But the astonishment was certainly not caused by the perfect entry of the projectile into the object, but because Antal had not been right in his own 'target' but in that of one of the rivals he had at his side. For this fateful mistake, the Hungarian was deducted 10 points, a penalty that, at the end of the day, was fatal. The gold medal was held by the Swedish Bertil Rõnnmark, who collected 294 points. Without the penalty, Barát-Lemberkovits, with existing 285 points, would have been champion. He finished in eighteenth place, among twenty-six participants.

AN UNFAIR MEDAL

The biggest win of field hockey in an official and international event took place on 11 August: India humiliated the United States with a score of 24–1. The historic match conferred the Asian team with gold, because a week earlier they had also thrashed Japan 11–1 in a just three-team tournament. The Japanese internationals, in turn, stayed with the silver after beating the local squad 9–2. From a modern perspective accustomed to current competitions, it can be very unfair to know that the United States recieved the bronze medal despite having made the worst campaign in the history of hockey with no wins, no draws, two losses, three goals scored and thirty-three conceded.

BERLIN 1936

'Sincere thanks to the competitors who have come from all over the world. They have filled us with admiration for their feats. Their names will last in the history of the sport. I express my hope that the Berlin Games have contributed to strengthening the Olympic ideal and cooperated to strengthen ties between people'. Who was the orator of this phrase of brotherly love between different nations and races? No, it's neitherPierre de Coubertin nor any Nobel Peace Prize winner, but Adolf Hitler. This sentence also amazes because it was pronounced on 16 August 1936, during the closure of the Berlin Olympiad, when in Germany, the country that was led by the Führer, most of the terrible laws against the Jewish citizens had already been approved. Among them, paradoxically, a rule on sports associations was issued that prevented the host nation from being represented, in its own Olympiad, by athletes of Hebrew origin. It is necessary to emphasise at this point that, when the IOC, chaired by the Belgian Henri de Baillet-Latour, voted in favour of the candidacy of Berlin, on 13 May 1931, the German government was not in the hands of Hitler, but of Heinrich Brüning, representative of a center coalition. National Socialism would consolidate in power two years later.

Hitler's speech, carefully prepared by his propaganda minister, Joseph Goebbels, was consistent with a wonderful Olympic Game from an organisational point of view. Delegations from all over the world—despite the call for boycotts of various humanitarian bodies—were awestruck in front of the majestic facilities specially prepared for the event. Newspapers from Argentina, France, England and Switzerland, among others, unanimously highlighted the pomp and pageantry that covered the Olympic Stadium and the other venues. The Germans even especially invited Spyridon Louis, winner of the 1896 Athens Marathon, who at sixty-five led the Greek delegation and climbed into the box to hand Hitler an olive bouquet brought directly from one of the sacred trees of Olympia. The German squad responded effectively to many preparations by obtaining the largest medal harvest: 38 golds, 31 silvers and 32 bronzes, well above the United States, which came in second place with 24 gold, 21 silver and 12 bronze medals.

Numerous publications highlighted the extraordinary feat of James 'Jesse' Owens, a descendant of African slaves born in Alabama who worked as a porter in the sumptuous Waldorf Astoria hotel in New York, who got four golden medals winning the 100 meters, 200 meters, the 4x100 relay and the long jump contest. It is said that the deed of Owens was a slap to the pride of the racist Nazis. Of course, Hitler did not celebrate the American feat with champagne, but he did not bother too much either. In the final medal count, in the eyes of the 'Führer', the greatness of the 'superior race' had been imposed.

RIGHT OF ADMISSION

On the first day of the competition, Hitler warmly received and conferred the record-breaker German shot-put winner, Hans Woellke—a police officer who would later be promoted to lieutenant for his services to his nation. Moments later, he welcomed and congratulated the Finn Irmari Salminen, winner of the 10,000 meters. However, the next day,

Hitler refused to greet the American Cornelius Johnson, a black athlete who had won the high jump contest. The 'Führer' claimed that he had to leave the stadium for an urgent state affair. The IOC president, the Belgian count Henri de Baillet-Latour, warned Hitler that he could not discriminate whom to congratulate in public or not, and that he should receive in his box all the competitors, or none. The local leader decided on 'none' and from that moment summoned his favourite athletes to his private office of the colosseum.

UNCOMFORTABLE CONGRATULATION

Adolf Hitler had fallen in love with the beauty of the American sprinter Helen Stephens, winner of the 100 meters on 4 August. In fact, Cupid's arrow had been so sharp that the Führer ordered one of his collaborators to invite the eighteen-year-old sprinter to visit him in his private Olympiastadion office. After the awards ceremony, the girl accepted the invitation, as she confessed, because she was 'curious' to personally meet the strong man from Germany 'everyone was talking about'. Stephens would soon regret being so inquisitive. According to her own account, the meeting began when the German leader received her with the traditional Nazi greeting. 'I gave him a good handshake, in the old Missouri style. Immediately, Hitler jumped into my jugular vein. He grabbed my butt, squeezed and pinched it, and then hugged me and in my ear he said: "You have a true Aryan guy. You should run to Germany". Then he gave me a shoulder massage and invited me to spend a weekend with him at his residence in Berchtesgaden'. Frightened, Stephens managed to escape from the office and the sticky Hitlerian harassment, and ran to take refuge among her countrymen. After winning the 4x100 relay, the young woman was invited again to Hitler's private room. This time, she accelerated in full speed, but to the opposite direction.

A FRIENDSHIP TOO PRECIOUS

James 'Jesse' Owens had stepped on the foul line in his first two attempts at the preliminary series of the long jump tournament in the morning of 4 August. If he committed a new error, he would have been eliminated from the competition. While the boy from Alabama waited for his next turn, he was approached by the German, Carl-Ludwig Long, a favourite to keep the gold. The German suggested the American start his jump several centimeters before, to avoid exceeding the limit line with his foot. Owens took note of the advice, and with the new technique, successfully completed the final chance and qualified for the next round. In the afternoon, after the elimination of the rest of the contestants, Long and Owens were 'side by side' in the contest for the gold medal. In his best attempt, the German made a great jump of 7.87 meters. The American, who closely followed the indication of his rival, flew to 8.06 meters, a new Olympic record that placed him in the first place on the podium. Long, far from getting angry at having created his own 'Frankenstein', was the first to congratulate the champion. Both athletes forged a brief but intense friendship, which was truncated by the Second World War : the German died in 1943 because of injuries received during a fight on the Italian island of Sicily. At the end of the war, Owens traveled to Leipzig to visit Long's family. 'You can melt down all the medals and cups I have and they wouldn't be a plating on the 24-carat friendship I felt for Luz Long at that moment,' said the great Berlin Olympic winner.

BRAVE HORSEMAN

The horse-riding contest (three-day event) combined different equestrian exercises: dressage, endurance and show jumping. This competition had both individual and team-wise participation, with three participants from each country. In Berlin, on the second day, several riders ended up on the ground. Fourteen of the eighteen teams had to give up the tournament due to the various injuries suffered by their competitors. One that had also fallen was the local Konrad von Wangenheim, who had a collarbone fracture. But instead of giving up, the courageous German decided to continue to help his team. The next day, with an arm tied to a sling, Von Wangenheim finished his routine despite the intense pain and suffering a second fall. The heroic knight did not score points, but having completed his journey, he managed to get the German team to keep the gold medal. Von Wangenheim's feat was copied twenty-four years later by Australian James William 'Billy' Roycroft, who also continued his routine with a broken collarbone to help his country win gold.

A POSSIBLE RACISM?

On 9 August, the head of the US track and field team, Lawson Robertson, took a particular decision: for the final of the 4x100 relay he decided to take out of the team Sam Stoller and Marty Glickman, boths Jews. This decision was highly criticised, since it was believed that Robertson, in this way, was consistent with the Nazi regime that dominated Germany. However, Stoller and Glickman were replaced by two African-American athletes, James 'Jesse' Owens and Ralph Metcalfe. Given Hitler's ethnic conception, who detested both Jews and blacks in the same way, it does not seem logical to accuse Robertson of being a racist. In addition, Owens and Metcalfe, along with the 'whites', Foy Draper and Frank Wycoff, not only won the race easily, but also achieved a new world record of 39.8 seconds. A register that, without a doubt, did not cause smiles for the Führer, especially after Germany was in the third place, surpassed also by the Italian quartet.

GOLDEN GLASSES

Italy was, in terms of titles, the best football team of the 1930s. The 'azzurri' squad, built by the master coach Vittorio Pozzo, won the two World Cups played that decade, Italy 1934 and France 1938, and also the Berlin Games tournament. For this competition, Pozzo called a striker as fulminant as particular: Annibale Frossi. Few fans celebrated the inclusion of Frossi, a man who had performed with little success in several clubs of the second division and who also had a low and thin body that did not fit the traditional football shape of the time. But above all these, the most striking thing was the fact that he used a thick pair of glasses to play. Yet despite all his peculiarities, the spectacle-guy not only was the great star and the top scorer of the championship developed in the German capital, but the main man behind Italy's returning home with the gold medal. Frossi scored the only goal that helped the 'azzurri' defeat the United States in the first game—a very violent match that ended with two Yankees retired by injury and an European sent off. He scored another hat-trick against Japan in the 8–0 quarter-final win, one against Norway in the semi-final that culminated in 2–1, and a brace against Austria—one of the greatest teams of that time—in the final match on 15 August at the Olympic Stadium, where the Italian team was crowned with the olive leaves before an audience of 85,000. After the Berlin success, Frossi went to Inter Milan, a team that won the titles of 1938 and 1940, and the Italian Cup of 1939, thanks to the goals by the man with the glasses.

HITLER'S ONLY FOOTBALL MATCH

Adolf Hitler did not like football. Moreover, according to some historians, he hated it. The Führer, who preferred athletic sports, more in line with his military passion and the integral development of the body, nevertheless accepted it as a prt of the Olympic tournament.

On 4 August, while Hitler enjoyed the track and field tests at the Olympiastadion, his propaganda minister Joseph Goebbels approached him, and in his ear, told him that a couple of kilometers away, in the Poststadion, the German team had just destroyed the Luxembourg 9–0. Goebbels told his boss that for many Germans, 'winning a game is more important than capturing a city in the East,' and convinced him to occupy the privileged seat in the Poststadion box three days later, when the strong German squad would face the supposedly weak Norway. Reluctantly, Hitler accepted, and on 7 August, attended the match with 55,000 of his countrymen. However, what seemed like a simple procedure for the locals became a Nordic hit. Seven minutes to the beginning, Magnar Isaksen beat the local goalkeeper Hans Jackob in the bewildered face of the Führer, who was looking at Goebbels for explanations. The nervous minister tried to apologise, but at 83 minute, Isaksen scored again to seal the Norwegian victory. While the visitors were celebrating the goal, the chancellor stood up from his seat, and throwing sparks and curses, escaped from the stadium followed by his minister and a waterfall of excuses. That was the only football match witnessed by Hitler.

A GIGANTIC ADVANTAGE

A few weeks before the start of the Games, the International Basketball Federation—founded just four years earlier in Geneva, Switzerland—ruled a strange regulation for the debut of this sport in the Olympics: the participating countries were forbidden to include players exceeding 1.90 meters in height in their teams. When the US coach James Needles came to know of the absurd decision, he almost died of a heart attack, since four of his stars—Ralph Bishop, Joe Fortenberry, Frank Lubin and Willard Schmidt—exceeded that level. Needles immediately submitted a letter to ask for the abolition of the ridiculous rule he considered discriminatory. After studying the writing and the solid arguments of the coach, FIBA had no choice but to cancel the measure.

But the surprises didn't end for Needles. Upon arriving in Berlin, the American discovered that the championship would take place on an outdoor court, on a ground covered with clay and sand. Anyway, these adverse conditions did not prevent the Yankees from reaching the final after crushing the Philippines 56–23 and Mexico 25–10, respectively. The culminating match, against Canada, was played after a storm that turned the field into a disaster. In the middle of the mud, the wind, a rain that appeared at times and with a soapy ball, it was impossible to hit the hoop from a long distance. The duel was defined in favour of the United States, precisely because of the advantage provided by its giants under the board. The squad of the stars and stripes took the gold medal for a meager score of 19–8 achieved on the abnormal pitch, and for the 'triple' scored by Needles at the FIBA desks.

THE FIRST 'REPLAY'

Just a few meters to reach the Automobil-Verkehrs und Übungs-Straße, the autodrome of the south of Berlin, the young Frenchman Guy Lapébie began to taste the victory in the individual cycling road race, held on 10 August 1936. Confronted with a tight competition on his right by his compatriot Robert Charpentier and on left by the Swiss Ernst Nievergelt, Lapébie led the final sprint with a slight advantage that seemed unrecoverable for his fiercest rivals. Already within the circuit, and with the finishing line a handful of centimeters away, the leader felt a pull on the left end of his jacket that slowed his dizzying march and allowed Charpentier to snatch the gold for two thousandths of a second. Lapébie could not believe what had happened to him. Furious, he got off his bike and pounced on Nievergelt with a bunch of thickest insults. The rage of the French could only be contained with the intervention of the judges, other cyclists, auxiliaries, journalists and even some spectators. When he calmed down, Lapébie approached Charpentier, gave him a handshake and assured him that 'the only thing that comforts me is that you were the winner'. 'If this shitty Swiss,' he continued, 'would not have pulled my shirt, without neglecting your triumph, I assure you that the victory had been mine'. At the end of the day, both had contributed to their country to keep the gold in the 'team' category of the same contest.

A few days later, in Paris, before traveling to his family home in Aquitaine, Lapébie took the opportunity to watch a movie in the theatre hall. Before the start of the film, the cyclist was surprised by beautiful clips from the different disciplines developed in the Games, broadcast by the film news bulletin. One of the shorts corresponded, precisely, to the final sprint of the cycling road race. When he paid attention to the images in which he appeared, Lapébie almost hit the ground with his jaw. He got fired from his armchair and started shouting to stop the tape and pass the cycling segment again. The athlete had to explain to the rest of the spectators and the theater employees that it was he who starred in the race, and that he wanted to observe his outcome again, but in slow motion, to corroborate if what he had just seen was indeed what he had thought. After several requests the technicians agreed to their demand. Lapébie was stunned by the images: frame by frame, it was clear that the hand that had truncated his victory was not of the Swiss, but of his fellow countryman, Charpentier. Thanks to the first 'replay' in history, Lapébie realised that he had committed an injustice. When crossing the Helvetian in the next race, the Frenchman explained what happened and apologised. Nievergelt accepted his apology and they began a deep friendship. The opposite happened with Charpentier: Lapébie never spoke to him again.

LONDON 1948

The terrible wounds caused by the Second World War had not yet healed when the IOC decided to carry out the 14th edition of the Games. For most of the sports federations, London 1948 was the fourteenth event, although only eleven tournaments had been played. Though Berlin 1916, Tokyo 1940 and London 1944 are listed as Olympic editions, there was no place for sports competition amidst bullets, bombs and deaths. The event developed on the English soil was the first since the end of hostilities in 1945 and is remembered as a tribute to the millions of dead left by the fateful conflict and as an extraordinary show of desire for world peace. Anyway, politics interfered into the Games. Germany was not invited, as in 1920, for being considered as the nation responsible for belligerence. Londoners were not willing to host the representatives of a nation that had bombed their land and their honour. Officially, however, it was indicated that in Germany there was no local government to send the official invitation. Regarding Japan, the IOC made sure that an invitation was sent but no one had responded. Meanwhile, two Israeli athletes, who had initially been accepted, were later marginalised following complaints from several Arab countries. Although the athletes were in London, it was argued that the country of the Middle East, flamingly constituted, did not have its Olympic committee. The rough diplomatic storm was not an easy task to handle for the Swedish Johannes Sigfrid Edström, the new president of the IOC after the death of Count Henri de Baillet-Latour. The Belgian leader had died from a heart attack in 1942, upon learning of the death of his son on the battlefront.

The London Games are also recognised as the austerity Olympiad. The serious world economic crisis, a consequence of the war, did not allow any luxury: the medals were not made of gold but of golden tin; everything was rationed, from food for athletes to transportation; though Wembley Stadium was refurbished with a lot of effort, no special Olympic Village was built: athletes were housed in various military camps (such as Uxbridge, West Drayton and Richmond) and schools such as Roehampton Southlands College, where the women were hosted. But the enormous energy of the English people and the fervour put by the athletes gave an extraordinary shine to the competition. The United States once again imposed itself on the medal table with 84 (38 golds, 27 silvers and 19 bronzes), followed by Sweden (46) and France (32).

LAND OF HUNGER

Three years after the end of the war, England was not in an ideal state to host an olympiad. The tremendous consequences of the conflict had not only left scars in the landscape of London—which was bombed by the Nazis—but also in its livelihood: almost half a million people died throughout the confrontation. The shortage of food was a serious problem for the 4300 athletes who intervened during the two weeks of the competition. Many of the delegations carried their own products to counteract hunger. Argentine athletes transported several tons of beef in their boat; the Americans arrived with 30 tons of beef, 6 of pork, 6 of lamb, 36 tons of cheese, 12 of sugar, 25,000 bars of chocolate, 600 liters of ice cream, half a ton of butter and 2400 dozens of eggs, and almost every day, they received hundreds of kilos of bread by air; the Swedes landed with 70 kilos of caviar and 180 kilos of pork; Denmark donated 200,000 eggs to the British Olympic Committee to distribute among competitors. France filled a train with different products, but after being delayed in British Customs, most of the food ended up decomposing. They did recover all the bottles of wine, which was supposed to serve each athlete more than a liter per day.

During the opening ceremony, it was officially reported that 7000 pigeons had been released.

Imported food was placed inside an old anti-aircraft shelter that served as a warehouse and was guarded day and night by about twenty volunteers, almost all of them students, armed with iron bars. Even a direct line with a police detachment was installed after a group tried to loot the pantry. Packaged fruits, meat, chocolate, tea, flour, wine, cheese, bacon, butter and condensed milk had a high value in the black market because of the huge demand.

Meanwhile, the Swiss female competitors complained about the poor quality of their meals and left their school hostels to stay at the Collingham Gardens Kensington Hotel on their own. Also the starving Danish swimmers called their relatives to beg to send them rations. Shortly before the start of the competition, the girls received 500 sandwiches that had been dispatched by plane. With a full belly, they got 2 golds and 2 silvers in only 5 tests: Karen-Margrete Harup was champion in the 100-meter backstroke; Greta Andersen, in 100-meter freestyle; Karen Margrethe Harup, second in the 400-meter freestyle; the complete team, silver in the 4x100 freestyle relay. This was the best number in the swimming history of Denmark (in the female catregory) until Moscow 1980. All thanks to some bread that, in post-war England, was not so little.

PIANO WOMAN

Micheline Ostermeyer displayed one of the best performances in the history of French athleticism in London. On 30 July, she won the gold in discus throw; on 4 August, she repeated the feat in the shot-put event with an Olympic record; On 7 August, she won the bronze medal in high jump. When a journalist asked her if she had trained intensively to achieve such excellence, Micheline replied: 'I practise athletics five hours a week, and five hours a day on the piano'. The champion, niece-granddaughter of the renowned French writer Victor Hugo and niece of the composer Luciano Paroche, was a distinguished concertist. The night before her first win, Ostermeyer offered a recital for her countrymen in an old piano at the Olympic Village; in that same instrument she celebrated her second gold, with the performance of a piece by Ludwig van Beethoven. For the girl, the sport was a break. First, during her studies at the conservatory; then, when embarking on her career as a professional musician. Micheline retired from athletic competitions in 1950, when she considered that these disciplines affected her reputation as a concert performer. She was so affected that for many years she refused to perform any composition of Franz Liszt. She considered them 'too sporty'.

BAREFOOT

The game between France and India on 31 August at the Lynn Road Stadium—home ground of the small London club Ilford, which was dismantled in 1976—may well be included in the gallery of the strangest football matches in history. India, which had never participated in an international competition outside Asia, presented a team with just barefooted players. This, in fact, should not have been accepted by the Swedish referee Gunnar Dahlner, since it violated the regulations about the outfit. However, the game was played. Contrary to what might be believed to be a serious disadvantage, due to grip and greater power at the shot, the lack of footwear was not noticed in the match process. The French, well planted in their boots, more experienced and with an extensive and intense football history, had to fight very hard against the unknown and impetuous rival team. The Gallic squad opened the score through René Courbin, but the Indians did not give up and matched the duel, thanks to a goal by Sarangapari Dhanraj Raman. Only five minutes from the end, the Swedish referee blew the whistle to award a penalty for Asians because of a strong foul inside the area. The execution was in charge of defender Sailendra Nath Maná, who took a violent shot that went wide of the goal defended by Guy Rouxel. Recovered from the shock and what could be a shameful situation, the Europeans regained control of the ball and they secured another goal, thanks to a successful shot by André Strape a minute from the final whistle. The joy, although over a bitter victory, lasted little for the Gallics: on 5 August they lost 0–1to England at Craven Cottage, the home of Fulham Football Club. The meager triumph against India would not be the only surprise that the French would suffer against the Asians: on 29 August 1960, during the Rome Olympic Games, the Indians, this time in shoes, achieved a historic tie in the Tuscan stadium of Grosseto.

Enthused by their surprising performance in London, the Asian team signed up to participate in the 1950 World Cup in Brazil. The draw placed them in Group 3 with Sweden, Paraguay and Italy. But as FIFA, which he had taken note of the irregularity occurred in England, stood firm and forbade to act barefoot; at the last moment India decided not to travel to South America. Faithful to the culture acquired in the streets of Delhi and Mumbai, the boys preferred to stay at home to trample their tradition.

WHAT A FORGET!

On the morning of 4 August, Pakistani Jaffar Ali Shah approached calmly on the edge of Wembley's Imperial Pool to particpate in the second preliminary heat. Seconds before the initial shot, Ali Shah took off his robe and, to his great surprise, discovered that he had forgotten to put on his swimsuit. Embarrassed in front of the spectators, the other participants and the judges, the Pakistani jumped into the water to hide his nudity. From the pool, Ali Shah requested that the race be delayed until one of his teammates approached his swimsuit. The organisers did not put any objection, especially because that test was, precisely, the 100-meter backstroke. After the unexpected inconvenience, the Pakistani said goodbye to the Games after finishing in the last position of the tie.

NEED FOR SPICE

According to several news sources, the organisers of the Games had to reinforce the security in the premise of the Southlands School, where the almost 300 foreign female athletes were staying, because during the first days 'numerous unauthorised visits' had been noticed. This measure caused some of the ladies to decide to change their accommodation. So much guard stifled. An IOC spokesperson tried to calm down the press interest on this situation by ensuring that 'invitations' to the school hostel had occurred because the athletes missed the typical foods of their respective countries, and in Southlands there were only tasteless dishes made by an English chef. Obviously, the girls needed a little more salt and pepper.

FROM WASHING THE DISHES TO BEING CHAMPION

The Dutch Fanny Blankers-Koen produced in London one of the biggest impacts in the history of athleticism. In Berlin 1936, at eighteen years,

Blankers-Koen had finished very far from the podium in high jump and in the 4x100 relay. But after the Second World War, twelve years and two children, this housewife became the first woman to obtain four gold medals in a single Game. The sprinter won the four-track contests she played: 100- and 200-, 80-meter hurdles (the last two with an Olympic record) and the 4x100 relay. When she returned to Holland after her fantastic performance, a customs agent asked her if she had 'something to declare'. 'Yes,' the champion replied proudly, 'four gold medals.' The inspector, happy to have met his heroine, remarked that 'they are only gold, but they should be diamonds'. Shortly after, during a ceremony in Amsterdam, the sprinter received a bicycle as a gift. With great modesty and a greater spirit, she thanked for the present obtained 'for running a few meters'. In 1999 she was chosen as the athlete of the 20th century by the International Association of Athletic Federations.

THE ROOKIE

Sergeant Károly Takács was the best shooter in the Hungarian army. The quality of his right hand was unmatched, invincible in every aiming competition. In 1936, Takács was proposed to be part of the team that would participate in the Berlin Olympics, but the Magyar leaders had to veto their candidacy for a regulatory inconvenience: for that sport, the Olympics were reserved only for officials. Far from being depressed, the young sergeant set out to continue the military career with fervour to achieve the necessary rank that would lead him to the Olympiad.

Two years later, during training, the Olympic dreams of the skillful sergeant were shattered by a defective grenade that exploded before being thrown by his right hand. The damage was devastating. Despite his invaluable loss, Takács was not defeated by adversity. He trained his left hand for months to make it respond as effectively as his right. Shortly before the 1948 London Games, in a pre-Olympic championship,

Takács, who had already ascended to lieutenant and reached all the requirements to travel to England, surprised his stunned rivals with a huge performance that put him back in first place of his country in the rapid-fire pistol category. When the Hugarian appeared at the National Shooting Center in the town of Bisley to compete, he met with Argentine participant Carlos Díaz Sáenz Valiente. Informed about the accident with the grenade, the South American shooter asked Takács, with a wry smile, why he had bothered to move to London. 'I came to learn,' replied the Magyar, proud of having fulfilled his Olympic dream. With a perfect performance, he not only won the gold medal but set a new world record. During the award ceremony, Díaz Sáenz Valiente, who had finished second and had to swallow his enormous pride, called Takács and respectfully admitted: 'I congratulate you. Apparently, you learned too much.'

The Hungarian feats continued in Helsinki 1952, when he established himself as the first shooter to win the pistol contest in two consecutive Olympics. In addition, he was the coach of his compatriot Szilárd Kun, who won the silver medal in the Finnish contest. Takács became a national hero and since then, he is synonymous with fight, effort and hope.

HELSINKI 1952

Helsinki was the breaking point of an Olympic hegemony. The entry of the Union of Soviet Socialist Republics (or Soviet Union or USSR, a conglomerate of European and Asian nations welded by communism that was born in 1922, consolidated after the Second World War and broke up in 1991, with the fall of the Berlin Wall) meant a huge blow to the United States. Until London 1948, the American team had shown its power without clouds on its horizon. In the Finnish capital, the Soviet Union warned Americans that the 'Cold War' between the West and the Communism would not only develop as a political, economic, ideological and military battle: it would also manifest itself strongly in the sporting arena. The USSR debuted with an excellent harvest of 22 golds, 30 silvers and 19 bronzes, a total of 71 medals that were just below the US production of 76—although 40 of those were golden. The Ukrainian gymnast Viktor Chukarin, with 4 gold medals, was the top champion of the Olympiad. With the running of different editions, until Barcelona 1992, the fight between the two political powers would steal the center of the sports scene.

The inauguration of the Games had as its main protagonist the magnificent Finnish Paavo Nurmi, designated to light the Olympic flame. Nurmi, who had gathered nine golds and three silvers between 1920 and 1928, had not been able to participate in Los Angeles 1932 for supposed 'professionalism'. His presence on the track of the Olympic stadium was a slap to the IOC to avenge an affront of two decades.

A GUARD TOO STRICT

To prevent any unwanted incident, the organisers of the Games arranged rigid security measures at the Olympic Stadium in Helsinki. The meticulous and extreme resolution included severe orders for the guards in charge of the spectators, entrances: 'Who has no entry or invitation card, does not pass. Without exception'. The custodians were so obedient that, before the Olympiad began, a serious inconvenience had already occurred. When the famous Paavo Nurmi arrived at the Colosseum to perform the last relay of the Olympic torch, a guard prevented his passage. 'I am Paavo Nurmi,' the former athlete blushed, surprised that he was not recognised by a compatriot. Nurmi had forgotten his card. Actually, he didn't carry it with him because he was dressed in a shirt and shorts without pockets. His sporting attire did not move the keeper, who stood firm: 'If you don't have your ticket, you can't enter'. The explanations were useless. Nurmi was desperate. His presence on the track was essential to slap the IOC, which had prevented him from intervening in Los Angeles 1932 after a complaint of alleged 'professionalism.' When his fervent desire for revenge seemed almost gone, an official from the local organisation passed by. Nurmi called him and the 'too efficient' guard was immediately ordered to let him pass. The veteran runner made his dream come true.

THE TABLE WAS WELL SERVED

After so many complaints regarding the scarcity of proper food in London 1948, both the organisers of the Olympiad and the various delegations took strong precautions to keep the athletes well satisfied.

To feed 5000 athletes from 69 countries, the Finns especially hired chefs from Japan, India, Pakistan, Norway, Brazil and Argentina for the dining rooms of the Olympic Village. The Italians and French, suspicious, decided to include in their delegations their own chefs, who prepared their delicacies in special units where their compatriots had lunch and dinner separated from the rest of the competitors. The Americans, meanwhile, included in their luggage 6000 steaks for the Olympic team, and every day they received by plane 1500 loaves of bread and 1000 kilos of ice cream, among other provisions.

IN THE NAME OF THE FATHER

William Havens had one foot on the ship that would transfer him to the 1924 Paris Games to participate in the tournament, in which he was a potential gold candidate. However, at the last moment, Havens decided to stay in Arlington, Virginia, to accompany his wife during the time of the birth of their second child. The dates of competition and the labor overlapped, forcing Bill to choose between one of the two important events of his life. He decided on his family.

Fate wanted the two sons of the rower, William Jr. and Frank, to participate in different Olympics. The older was fifth in the Canadian single 1000 meters in London 1948; the youngest won silver medal in the Canadian single 10,000 meters in the same edition. The Havens family was very happy, although Frank felt that his contribution had not been enough. On 27 July 1952, on the Taivallahti canal in Helsinki, again in the 10,000-meter contest, Frank Havens beat the young Hungarian Gábor Novák by eight seconds and finally got the gold that the family so longed for. As soon as he received his prize, the boy ran to send a telegram to his father: 'Dear Dad. Thank you for staying to wait for my birth in 1924. I return home with the gold medal. You deserved one. Your beloved son, Frank'.

AMAZON

Danish horsewoman Lis Hartel made a magnificent performance on 29 July at the Ruskeasuo equestrian center that allowed her to win the silver medal in the individual dressage contest, behind the Swedish Henri Saint Cyr but ahead of distinguished male colleagues. Four years later, Hartel doubled her silver, again surpassed only by Saint Cyr. The skill of the danish left everyone open-mouthed, and it was not because of her sex: as a result of a polio attack when she was twenty-three years old, the Nordic rider had her two legs paralysed below the knees. Hartel even had to be helped to get on and off her efficient horse, Jubilee. The woman took advantage of the popularity gained on the track to create a foundation to fight against polio.

DAD'S DIVE

Frenchman Jean Boiteux came from a family of swimmers. His father Gaston had participated in numerous open water competitions; his mother, Bienna Pellegry, had represented France in the 1924 and 1928 Olympics. On 30 July, so much passion for water overflowed Mister Gaston: seeing his son having won the gold medal in the 400-meter freestyle, the man, out of control and fully clothed, ran down from the stand and jumped into the pool to embrace his boy in a very damp celebration. For the happy father, Jean's Olympic record was well worth the extravagant performance.

FROM HERO TO SWEEPER

Each Game has its huge star and in Helsinki the greatest was Emil Zátopek. The Czech achieved a tremendous athletic feat which seems unrepeatable: in just one week he won the gold medal in the 5000 meters, the 10,000 meters and the marathon. Moreover, on 24 July, his own wife Dana Zátopková won the gold in javelin throw contest minutes after his victory in the 5000 meters. On 20 July, after crediting his first victory in the10,000 meters, Zátopek perplexed the journalists: 'I was not fast, it was not a very good race'. He had just broken the Olympic record he had achieved in London 1948 in almost 43 seconds.

A week later, the Czech, who had never participated in a marathon, set out to fight the great crown with the Englishman James Peters, the favourite and the record-holder. Zátopek and Peters led the race from the start. Near 15 kilometer, he asked his British rival: 'I never ran a marathon. Are we doing well with this rate?' Peters replied that it was 'a little slow'. 'A little slow? Then we have to accelerate a Little,' Zátopek said and increased his speed. The English was so demoralised that he left shortly after. Without opposition, the 'Prague Beast' reached the final line after 2 hours, 23 minutes and 3 seconds, a new Olympic mark. The second, the Argentine Reynaldo Gorno, arrived two and a half minutes later, while Zátopek ate an orange. The Czech approached the South American, congratulated him and offered him a slice. After the awards ceremony, he told reporters that 'the marathon is a very boring race'.

When he returned to his country, the runner was promoted to colonel by the communist government that was sponsored by the Soviet Union. In 1968, during the popular uprising called 'Prague Spring', Zátopek—an idol of great prestige in his country—signed the manifesto of the reformer Alexander Dubcek, who intended to change the regime that ruled the nation. The Soviets took note of the athlete's political position and when they regained control over Czechoslovakia, degraded him from colonel to sweeper. Discredited by the red media apparatus, the Helsinki hero was submerged in a terrible misery. He could only resurface in 1975, after paying the high cost of a public apology to the invaders.

MELBOURNE 1956

Everything comes to an end. Melbourne was the 'Waterloo' of the American Olympic hegemony. Although the US team had resigned from the first place of the medal board on three previous occasions, it had always been surpassed by host countries: by France in Paris 1900, by Great Britain in London 1908 and by Germany in Berlin 1936. In the remaining eight Games, the American squad had easily imposed on its rivals. In Australia, the Yankees again demonstrated their supremacy in athletic events, with 16 golds, 10 silvers and 5 bronzes. However, the Games are much more than track and field competitions, and the final statistics established a new Olympic champion: The Soviet Union. The red team added 98 medals (37 golds), much more than the Americans who bagged 74 medals (32 golds). The USSR contingent was almost unbeatable in sports such as gymnastics, canoeing, weightlifting and wrestling (greco-roman and freestyle), and stood out in disciplines such as football, shooting and fencing, most popular in Western Europe.

Melbourne suffered the first significant Olympic boycotts, generated by several ongoing political conflicts such as the one that happened between the Soviet Union and Hungary, two nations of the communist bloc, or the Sinai War (or Suez Crisis) that put Egypt against Israel, France and England. This conflagration caused the defection of Egypt, Iraq and the Republic of Lebanon. China, meanwhile, said its absence in Oceania was due to the fact that the IOC had accepted that Taiwan compete as an independent nation, despite being under its sovereignty.

One of the most curious matters of these Games was based on the strict livestock policies of Australia. As in that state there was a rigid disposition that forced all imported animals to remain an extensive quarantine period to prevent the spread of diseases, equestrian competitions (six tests, with few participating countries, basically European) were carried out in Stockholm, the Swedish capital, more than 15,000 kilometers from the Australian headquarters and five months before the official opening at the Melbourne Cricket Club stadium. The 1956 Olympic was the only Olympiad in history that was staged in two different countries.

USSR–HUNGARY AND THE FIRST MASSIVE BOYCOTT

Just a month before the Games, the Soviet army invaded Budapest to crush a popular revolutionary movement that tried to modify the harsh policies imposed by Moscow on Hungary, one of its 'satellite' nations behind the 'iron curtain'. More than a thousand tanks circulated through the streets of the Hungarian capital and in just over two weeks put the resistance under the red boot. The revolt ended with 2500 Hungarians dead, thousands of detainees and 20,000 exiles. Knowing what happened in Budapest, Spain, Switzerland and the Netherlands decided not to share the sporting event with the USSR. The unusual thing is that after all these, Hungary did intervene, the country directly affected by the political conflict.

NEVER FAVOURITE, ALWAYS WINNER

The American discus-thrower Alfred Oerter has a privileged place in the Olympic hall of fame. He was present in four Games—Melbourne 1956, Rome 1960, Tokyo 1964 and Mexico 1968—never as a favourite, but he always returned to New York with two prizes: a gold medal and an Olympic record. Oerter's outstanding career began in Australia, when he was twenty years old. Totally unknown, he joined the Olympic team becuase of the injury of a teammate. However, his 56.36 meter-hurl was unattainable for the rest of the competitors. By Rome 1960, Oerter had been overshadowed by his compatriot Richard Babka, who had broken the world record a month before the Games. In addition, he was not believed to have recovered fully from the injuries caused by a car accident that occurred on 5 October 1957. However, the Olympic gods once again favoured the New Yorker: his 59.18 shot exceeded Babka's by more than 1 meter. In Tokyo 1964, the bets did not accompany Oerteragain: not only he did face the Czech Ludvík Danek, at that time the new record-holder, but he had arrived at the Games with a pair of broken ribs and a damaged cervical disc that forced him to use an orthopedic neck. To top it all, in one practice he slipped on the wet ring and broke a costal cartilage. To train, all he could do was walk from the Olympic Village to the Tokyo national stadium. On 15 October, despite so many setbacks, the New Yorker took off his annoying orthopedic neck for a moment and threw his then career-best register of 61 meters for his third Olympic record, to the amazement of the crowd and the Czechoslovakian Danek, who believed himself unbeatable but was relegated to the silver medal. For Mexico 1968, it was presumed that the legend would end with the American Jay Silvester, who had triumphed in twenty of the twenty-two contests that had been developed that year. But Oerter threw his piece up to 64.78 meters for a new triumphant double. 'These are the Olympic Games, one dies for them,' said the first man to win four gold medals in four consecutive editions. The great discobolus left the sport in 1969 to raise his two daughters, although he continued with the practice of his beloved discipline. He retired when he got his best brands: on 31 May 1980, at the age of forty-three, he released the discus at 69.46 meters. If he had traveled to the Moscow Games that year, with that distance he would have quintupled his gold. Of course, the foreign policy of the United States would not have allowed it, because it had promoted a boycott against the Moscow edition. Oerter's story continued in September 1982, when he was summoned to record some images for the ESPN channel. At forty-five, he released the discus up to 73.15 meters. If it had been an official contest, he would have achieved the new world record.

COFFEE WITH JAVELIN

In his first game, the Norwegian Egil Danielsen was very nervous. In the qualifying round of the javelin throw event, played on the morning of 26 November, he had made many mistakes and his shots were very far from his best marks. He was placed for the finals miraculously by a few centimeters. Shortly before the start of the decisive round, Danielsen's insecurity was observed by his French colleague Michel Macquet, who approached him to offer him a coffee. The Norwegian didn't usually drink that infusion, but he accepted the invitation anyway. Loaded with caffeine, the Nordic athlete calmed down and greatly improved his performance, to the point that his latest throw was set at 85.71 meters, a new world record. Seeing the spectacular work of Danielsen, the French also tried to fill himself with black liquid, but nothing was left in the pot. The last cup had been drunk by the champion. The Norwegian took the gold and Macquet barely reached seventh place, far from the podium.

FOUR MEDALS IN THREE CONTESTS

The exceptional Soviet rower Vyacheslav Ivanov won the three races of single sculls in which he participated—Melbourne 1956, Rome 1960 and Tokyo 1964—and received 4 gold medals. The arithmetic operation is correct, dear reader: 4, because in Australia he received 2. On 27 November, after defeating Australian Stuart MacKenzie and American Jack Kelly in the final, the eighteen-year-old Muscovite athlete collected his first golden medal. Ivanov was so excited about his prize that, as soon as he stepped off the podium, he picked the medal up to show it to his teammates waiting for him at the dock. But the Soviet, still trembling with emotion, stumbled and his elusive medallion fell to Lake Wendouree. Desperate, the boy jumped into the water to recover his beloved reward, but failed to find it. The crying and deep disappointment of the young rower moved the IOC delegates, who agreed to give him a second gold to replace the one that was buried at the bottom of the lake.

STEEL ARM

In addition to starring in a very particular wedding, Connolly stood out for a physical defect that helped him become an Olympic champion. Due to a congenital problem, the athlete's left arm had not developed normally, and was more fragile and 10 centimeter shorter than the right. During his childhood, the American fractured thirteen times that member playing football and other sports, until a teacher in his school advised him to practise hammer-throwing to strengthen it. Over the months, the limb became stronger and acquired a slight curvature that favoured the shots. Classified for the Games, Connolly knew that his great rival in Melbourne would be the Belarusian Mikhail Krivonosov, European champion in 1954 and who had broken the world record seven consecutive times. When he began preparing to travel to the Games, the American placed a photo of the Soviet in the rearview mirror of his car as an incentive to keep his burning hunger alive for the golden target. The arduous training and concentration got Connolly to throw the hammer at 68.54 meters in a preparatory tournament for the Olympics.

That distance was more than 1 meter longer than Krivonosov's best record in his last official presentation. A colleague asked if he was ready to remove the photo from the mirror of the vehicle. 'Not yet,' he replied. On the morning of the competition, on 24 November, the American showed up very early in the Melbourne Cricket Club Stadium. His objective? To help his excellent preparation with a small psychological ploy. Connolly made some marks—about 72 meters from the launch semicircle, a distance far greater than the world record. The Soviets took the bait and got demoralised. Krivonosov failed in his last three throws and his best shot had barely reached 63.03 meters. Connolly secured the gold with 63.19 meters. A new Olympic record with which, finally, he was able to remove the photo from his car.

THE MIMOUN AWARDS

Algerian French Alain Mimoun O'Kacha crossed the finishing line, but barely celebrated his victory in the marathon. Mimoun stood by the arrival demarcation to wait for his great friend and until then relentless rival Emil Zátopek. Three times he had faced the Czech 'side by side' and in all he had to settle for the silver medal: in the 10,000 meters of London 1948 and Helsinki 1952, and in the 5000 meters of the Helsinki 1952. Four and a half minutes later, the 'Prague locomotive'—who had been operated from a hernia six weeks before the Games—finally appeared. 'Congratulate me!', the Algerian demanded with a smile. 'I am an Olympic champion!' Radiant and very proud of his friend, Zátopek approached and joined the brand new winner in a big hug. 'For me, this has been better than the medal,' Mimoun assured the Czech in a whisper in his ear. Gold and Zátopek's warm gesture were not the only gifts the champion received that December. A journalist from the Parisian sports newspaper *L'Equipe* notified the African runner that he had been father of a girl the day before. As soon as he was able to talk over telephone to his wife, who was in Paris, the first thing Mimoun asked to her was to baptise the little girl as 'Olympia'.

FORBIDDEN SOUVENIR

The favourite souvenir of the athletes who performed in Melbourne was the 'boomerang', the traditional throwing weapon of the aboriginals of Australia. This device has a remarkable physical characteristic: due to its aerodynamic design made of specially curved wood, once thrown, it can fly and return to the starting point. With the help of local athletes, many visitors acquired their boomerangs and learned to use them for fun. But unfortunately, they were not instructed very well: the organisers of the Games had to ban the boomerangs inside the Olympic Village after several glass windows got shattered.

ROME 1960

The 'Eternal City' put all its history and beauty at the disposal of the Games. Splendid monuments such as the Colosseum, the Arch of Constantine, the Baths of Caracalla and the Via Appia were some of the scenarios that served as a lavish framework for an Olympic that was considered the most luxurious one organised until then. To take advantage of the magnificent views and the numerous historical sites, the marathon was developed through a circuit over the old city center. The race began in Piazza di Campidoglio at 5:30 pm and ended, at night, under the Arch of Constantine, located between the Colosseum and the legendary forum. It was a glamorous Olympiad in every detail. According to journalists John Kieran and Arthur Daley, at the opening ceremony held at the Stadio Olimpico, only the most slender and beautiful athletes were allowed to parade. 'Since not even Dior could have done much with the heavy muscular girls, all the put-throwers were left in the Olympic Village. Just slender, young and beautiful people were exposed to the spectators.'

ROYAL CHAMPION

Prince Constantine of Greece won a gold medal in the Dragon-class regatta with his Niref boat, along with his teammates, Odyssevs Eskitzoglou and Georgios Zaimis. As is the tradition at the end of the race, the twenty-year-old athlete was pushed into the water…by his mother, Queen Frederika. Meanwhile, Hungarian fencer Aladár Gerevich participated in his sixth consecutive Olympiad with a unique performance: in all of them he won gold with the sabre team. Gerevich, who was present at the Games from 1932 to 1960, was also gilded in the individual sabre contest in London 1948, and also added a silver and two bronzes. In Rome, the remarkable swordsman was fifty years old.

The Soviet Union once again prevailed in its politics–sports duel with the United States, this time by a margin greater than that of in Melbourne: 103 medals (43 golds) to 71 (34 golds).

LACONIC

On 25 August, minutes before the official opening of the Games, the organisers distributed the press copies of the extensive speeches planned by the presidents of Italy and the IOC, Giovanni Gronchi, and the American Avery Brundage, respectively, during the ceremony. But when they were in front of the microphone, Gronchi and Brundage barely expressed a few words. The local president, for example, only said 'I declare the Games of the XVII Olympiad inaugurated,' much less than what was planned. When reporters asked the IOC press officers what had happened to the program, they responded that the ceremony had been shortened due to the intense heat. With 33°C recorded that day, it was feared that Gronchi, seventy-three years old and wrapped in a suit as ordered by the protocol, would end up dehydrated after an extensive speech.

A NEW IDENTITY

Cassius Marcellus Clay thought that the gold medal he had been awarded at the Palazzo dello Sport would give him a fair and long-awaited halo of respect back home. The boxer, who won the light-heavyweight category, kept his precious jewel hanging several days on his chest, to show the whole world the fruit of his Roman feat. However, the first night when he tried to enter into a fine restaurant in Louisville, his hometown in the state of Kentucky, his golden shield was useless: he was not allowed to enter because he was a black man. Disconsolate, he walked to a bridge over the Ohio river and threw the medal into the water. Clay had represented a country that turned its back on him. In retaliation, later he would embrace the Muslim faith and a new identity which replaced his 'slave name': Muhammad Ali. He would become the greatest boxer in the history.

HE WHO CAME FIRST, GOT A SILVER

The final of the 100-meter freestyle men's competition held on the night of 26 August at the Stadio Olimpico del Nuoto generated one of the biggest controversies in Olympic history. The race was won by the American Lance Larson in such a tight contest that the judges ended up serving the gold medal to the Australian John Devitt. The margin was so little that three controlling referees saw Larson as a winner, and the other three, Devitt. An electronic timer had been released in the Roman pool, which was only planned in case of a controversial end. Faced with the controversy, the chief judge, the Swedish Henry Runströmer, resorted to the device, which gave the American a time of 55.12, while the Australian, 55.16. However, after a long deliberation, Runströmer dismissed the electronic records and imposed his capricious stance: he claimed to have seen Devitt win. The unusual thing is that, officially, both were designated co-owners of a new Olympic record of 55.2 seconds. The United States team appealed, but a committee led by Dutchman Jan de Vries rejected the demand and kept the gold for the Australian. Indignant, the Treasurer of the American Olympic Committee, Max Ritter, filed countless complaints for four years, all dismissed. For Larson there was at least one consolation a week later, when he obtained the gold in the 4x100-meter medley relay, in which he swam the butterfly style. Yet, he could hardly avenge his snatched glory since Dewitt was not parto f the Australian team that came second.

BAREFOOT MARATHON RUNNER

Adidas, the German-based clothing company, sponsored the 1960 Olympics as the 'official footwear', which offered shoes for free to competitors who needed new running shoes. However, when the Ethiopian Abebe Bikila went to look for a pair to participate in the marathon, he did not find one that fit his big pair of feet comfortably. Without proper shoes, Bikila made an unusual determination: running 42,195 meters barefoot. As his soles were accustomed to plow through the roughest African soil, the athlete that had arrived in Rome by chance due to the injury of a compatriot, surprised with an unexpected triumph, which set a new world record on the cobbled streets of the eternal city illuminated by a huge moon. After his triumphant crossing of the Arch of Constantine, in front of the majestic Colosseum, the champion took advantage of his moment of glory to 'avenge' the oppressed forty years his nation was subdued by Italian power, half of that time under the regime of Benito Mussolini. Italy freed its prey at the end of the Second World War. 'I wanted to tell to the world that my country, Ethiopia, has always won with determination and heroism,' Bikila said. But the homeowners had their 'vendetta': during the awards ceremony, the musicians of the official band, who did not know the anthem of Ethiopia, performed the Italian national song.

HOT TRAINING

The bad performance in Melbourne, where he had not been able to complete the 50-kilometer race, forced the English walker Donald

Thompson to take extreme measures. He wanted a medal at all costs. A full, thorough training was not enough for the 1960 Games. He had to do something else to face excellent rivals such as New Zealander Norman Read and Swede John Ljunggren (gold and bronze, respectively, in Australia) and the sticky Roman summer. After analysing the situation and discussing with doctors and trainers, Thompson equipped one of the rooms in his house with stoves and pots with boiling water that created an oppressive atmosphere. For months, the English exercised several hours each day in the midst of the soporific environment of heat and humidity. The sacrifice yielded good results: Thompson not only won the contest from beginning to end, but also achieved a new record time of 4 hours, 25 minutes and 30 seconds.

THE HELPLESS POLICE

The Roman experience could not be worse for the Australian boxer Ronald Taylor. The fighter, who served as a detective for the Melbourne City Police, was knocked out by the American Percy Price in the second round of the first fight of maximum weight in the Palazzo dello Sport. When he returned to the Olympic Village, the agent discovered with annoyance that an anonymous thief had taken advantage of his absence to enter and seize 200 pounds he had kept in his suitcase. Doubly defeated, the policeman embarked on the first flight to quickly forget his humiliating passage through the Games.

WATER AND ALCOHOL

Something was wrong at the swimming stadium on the morning of 30 August. While seven competitors struggled with the aim of qualifying for the 400-meter freestyle final, the Soviet Leonid Kolesnikov splashed an unusual and zigzagging 'doggy' style. The judges intervened immediately and ordered Kolesnikov, a boy of Uzbek origin, to leave the pool before he crashes any participant. Upon leaving the water, the referees discovered that the Soviet was completely drunk, so they asked the red team managers to take care of him. After two days of sleeping in the Olympic Village, Kolesnicov returned to the pool for the 4x100 medley relay. However, his sober contribution was poor: Soviet Union was in fifth place.

THE SLEEPING BEAUTY

For this edition, the small South American state of Suriname decided to send its first Olympic athlete, runner Siegfried Willem Esajas. Esajas was registered to compete in the 800-meter contest. But, on the morning of 31 August, the young Surinamese did not appear for his qualifying dash because...he had fallen asleep! Esajas had gone to rest the night before convinced that the first races were scheduled for the afternoon. When he finally arrived at the Colosseum and learned of his mistake, he started crying like a baby. His colleagues, malicious, baptised him 'the sleeping beauty'.

A DANGEROUS RESCUE

The chronicles of the time highlight a situation as curious as it was funny on 30 August at the Stadio Olimpico del Nuoto, during the women's final of the 100-meter butterfly. After the start, the American Carolyn Wood, a fourteen-year-old girl, stopped her swimming after traveling about 30 meters and clung to the rope that delimited the lanes. One version indicated that she had accidentally swallowed water; while to another, she had suffered a cramp; a third, that she had not been able to overcome the nerves of the debut. Whatever be the reason, the outcome was nothing short of hillarious. While she was attached to the cable, a spectator who believed she was in danger, jumped fully dressed in the water to rescue her. The teenager, surprised as she recovered, began to swim in the opposite direction to escape from her mad saviour. Overcome the bad moment, Wood returned to the pool on 2 and 3 September to win with her team two golds in the 4x100 freestyle and 4x100 medley relays, respectively.

HE BREAKS, HE BENDS, BUT HE NEVER GIVES UP

'You can't leave. You have a broken collarbone and a dislocated shoulder,' the doctors warned Australian James William 'Billy' Roycroft, who had been hospitalised after falling from his horse. The doctors even threatened to hide the riding clothes, but it was useless. 'I ride in underpants,' the fearless rider replied firmly. Roycroft signed a note admitting that he was leaving the healthcare center against the advice of his doctors, whom he would also dissociate from any eventual consequences. Fractured, beaten, hurt and clogged with painkillers, Billy went to the stadium to finish what he had started two days before: the tournament that combined jumps, cross country and dressage, over three days. Roycroft did not seek personal glory, but the triumph of his country. Dressed and put on the horse by his companions, Lawrence Morgan, Neale Lavis and Brian Crago, Billy completed his routine bent of pain on the back of the animal and without sensation in his right arm. The immense effort was not in vain, because his feat allowed the Australian quartet to return to Oceania with the gold medal.

TOKYO 1964

The celebration of the Tokyo Games showed that an event of global significance does not necessarily need the European or American hand. Until this edition, the Games had traveled only to Europe and countries of Anglo-Saxon tradition, such as the United States and Australia. The Japaneses were prestigious hosts and fulfilled their goal as the most meticulous among all their predecessors. About eleven years after the end of the Second World War, which had Japan on the losing side, the nation of the 'rising sun' stood up and even had the pleasure of taking a small revenge in the best Finnish style: the person in charge of lighting the Olympic Flame was Yoshinori Sakai, a nineteen-year-old boy born in Hiroshima on 6 August 1945, the most infamous day in their history when an inhuman atomic bomb fell on that city (and three days later, that would be repeated in Nagasaki).

On the sporting level, an interesting controversy arose: the Soviet Union accumulated 96 medals, 6 more than the United States, but the Yankees gathered more golds, 36 against 30. This generated a spicy discussion about which country had been the 'champion' of the Olympiad. This consideration still remains unresolved, because a ranking is not officially made based on a score assigned to each medal, depending on its colour. On this subject, the *New York Herald Tribune* newspaper published a particular analysis: for the journal, which disappeared in 1967, the great winner 'per capita' of the Japanese Olympiad was Bahamas, which added only 1 gold medal, obtained in the Tornado yachting class. The peculiar observation was based on the fact that the population of Bahamas—an archipelago located in the Atlantic Ocean close to Cuba and Miami—had, at that time, was 108,200. According to the *New York Herald Tribune*, the United States, then inhabited by just over 190 million people, must have added 1790 gold medals to match Bahamian success. 'They have been the real winners of the Tokyo Olympiad. A real sporting threat just 50 miles from our shores,' the newspaper said ironically.

Regarding the hero of the Games, there were no controversies: the American swimmer Donald Arthur 'Don' Schollander added 4 golds in the 100- and 400-meter freestyle, and the 4x100 and 4x200 relays, also freestyle. In the first of his successes, Schollander broke the Olympic record, and in the following three, the world mark.

The flagpole with the Olympic emblem became a metaphor for the hosting nation, which was hoisted inside the stadium. The post was 15.21 meters high, the same distance Mikio Oda had achieved in Amsterdam 1928, when he won the first Olympic gold medal for Japan in the triple jump.

EMPLOYEE OF THE MONTH

One grandson of Emperor Hirohito, Nobuhiko Higamahinuki, worked in the Olympic Village as a dishwasher. The nineteen-year-old boy and a student at Keio University, in Tokyo, enrolled as a volunteer to enjoy sports fever, practise the languages he had studied and also learn something from other dialects. Son of the imperial princess Shigeko, Hirohito's eldest daughter, Nobuhiko assumed his cleaning duties like any commoner, and with great care he showed up at 6:30 am every day to take care of the sponge and detergent for nine long hours.

SELF-PUNISHMENT

The female javelin throw event had a surprising outcome. The great favourite was the Soviet national, Elvira Ozolina, champion in Rome Olympic, holder of the current world record (61.38 meters) and winner of the 1962 European championship. But her performance in Tokyo was very poor—she could not even get close to 60 meters—and was fifth, away from the podium led by the Romanian, Mihaela Penes. Depressed by her dismal performance, Ozolina went to the hairdresser in the Olympic Village and demanded that the employee shave her head. The hairdresser, frightened by the shaken face of the voluminous athlete, refused to comply with the order. Elvira, determined to punish her ineptitude, took the shaving machine and began to cut all her hair with her own hand. When she noticed the damage, the hairdresser agreed to level the mess. The Soviet athlete left the hairdresser's room completely bald and walked throughout the Olympic Village.

IMPERIAL JOKE

A successful Australian swimmer Dawn Fraser, winner of a gold medal (in the 100-meter freestyle) and a silver medal (in the 4x100 freestyle relay) did not satisfy her whim of souvenir. Fraser, who added four golds and four silvers between Rome and Tokyo, decided to take as a souvenir nothing less than a flag of the Japanese imperial palace. During a walk along with few others, the famous athlete passed over the security bars and seized a huge white pavilion with the five intertwined Olympic rings that flew over the grand residence. However, the crime did not go unpunished. The intrusion was detected by the guards, and Fraser was arrested by a police patrol. The news generated a scandal in the Olympic Village. The Australian Swimming Federation felt such humiliation that it decided to suspend Dawn for ten years, despite the fact that the girl had been pardoned by Emperor Hirohito himself in person, who had also given her the stolen flag. Although months later the punishment was reduced to four years, Fraser determined to withdraw from the official competitions, angry with the Federation officers. She considered they had been more 'imperialist' than the Emperor.

REFEREES PUNISHED

One of the black spots in the history of the Games was marked by two boxers, one Spanish and one Argentine, who instead of standing out for fighting against their rivals, put their names in the bad-book of the Olympic for hitting the referees. The first case occurred on 13 October, during a first-round fight of the featherweight category, between the Iberian Valentín Loren and the Chinese Hsu Hung-Cheng. Enraged by the verdict of the Hungarian referee Gyórgy Sermer, who had given the victory to the Oriental, Loren pounced on the judge and punched him with an accurate hit to the jaw. The spectators, taken aback, commented that he would undoubtedly have won his fight, and probably the gold medal, if he had had the same precision during the competition. Loren, who was eighteen, was suspended for life from all official combats, and was expelled from the Olympic Village with his coach. Three days later, the light middleweight Argentine José Chirino assaulted the Egyptian referee, Kosey Maghaby after a point was deducted in a second round fight. Chirino, who had defeated the Jamaican John Elliott in his debut, was disqualified, and the victory was awarded to the Soviet national Boris Lagutin, who would later win a gold medal. The Argentine only received a penalty of three years, because his attack had not been as violent as Loren's and because, in addition, he had the decency to apologise to his victim before retiring from the ring.

TRIUMPH OF LIFE

The Swedish brothers Lars Gunnar Käll and Stig Lennart Käll received medals from the IOC, but not for their participation in the yachting 'Flying Dutchman' race, held in Enoshina Bay. The Nordic navigators were awarded for their sporting nobility, because they abandoned the competition to help their Australian rivals, Ian Winter and John Dawe, whose boat was capsized. The Swedish rescued the Australians from the waters and also helped them to rebuild their ship, Diablo. Then both teams continued the race, with a very interesting result: Winter and Dawe finished in the fourteenth place, while the Käll brothers arrived later, ranked eighteen. There was no podium for the blue and gold flag but there was the pride of winning the Fair Play Award, delivered by the IOC for the very first time.

HISTORY REPEATS ITSELF

Although he had won several marathons after his great appearance in Rome, the Ethiopian international, Abebe Bikila, did not arrive in the Japanese capital as the favourite. His resistance was in doubt, because six weeks before the Games, he had undergone a surgery for appendicitis. But the African athlete ran in full force on 21 October. This time, wearing Puma's brand shoes, Bikila not only won with absolute comfort but also lowered the world record at 2 hours, 12 minutes and 11 seconds. The African doubled his Olympic gold, but the official band of the Tokyo National Stadium also repeated the Roman history—the musicians did not know the anthem of Ethiopia; the orchestra performed the national song of the host country.

THE SAD END

The bronze medal of the marathon was won by the local athlete Kokichi Tsuburaya. The third place was celebrated with much emotion by the

75,000 spectators who filled the national stadium, since Japan did not get a track and field medal since Berlin 1936. However, Tsuburaya was not happy at all. The Japanese had reached the finishing line more than 4 minutes after the winner, the Ethiopian Abebe Bikila, although with good chances to keep the silver medal. But, in the last meters, Tsuburaya lost his pace and the second place was taken by the British national, Basil Heatley, who until that day was the holder of the world record. That night, the local runner confessed to his roommate Kenji Kimihara, 'I have made an unforgivable mistake before the whole country. I will only get forgiveness if I win the gold in Mexico and enter the stadium waving the Japanese national flag.' The next three years, Tsuburaya had a kind of obsession to achieve his objective. But his destiny was far from the gold medal. In the first days of January 1968, while training in a Japanese sports center, the marathoner suffered the rupture of the achilles tendon of his right ankle. On 9 January, the day after the doctors told him that he would not recover in time to compete in the Mexican capital, Tsuburaya committed suicide after cutting the carotid artery with a razor blade. Before taking the desperate decision, the athlete wrote a brief note: 'I can't run anymore'. In his hometown, Sukagawa, a marathon is still held every year in his memory.

PEACEFUL FIGHTER

South Korean boxer Dong Kih Choh had arrived in Tokyo with high expectations of getting a medal in the flyweight category. In the first match, he defeated Iranian national, Nasser Aghai by disqualification. Then the Filipino, Dominardo Caminarde by a fair margin of points. But against the Soviet Stanislav Sorokin, Kih Choh was eliminated by the referee, who thought that he bent his head too low, below the height of his rival's belt. The Korean did not accept the verdict of the judge, and instead of leaving the ring, he sat in his corner and began a strike in protest of his disqualification. Kih Choh stayed 51 minutes on his stool, until a delegate convinced him to depose his attitude. The claim took a prominent place in the newspapers of the time because, unlike the Spanish Vicente Loren or the Argentine Roberto Chirino, the eastern fighter had opted for a non-violent protest.

MEXICO 1968

Like its traditional food, Mexico organised a very spicy tournament. In sports, the main seasoning was provided by the height of the city, located about 2200 meters above sea level. The lower atmospheric pressure and the reduced amount of oxygen allowed records to be broken in short-distance contests, but none in long-lenght competitions. Another bit of pepper was brought by some regulatory changes. For this edition, the IOC included sex and doping controls. The first 'positive' case corresponded to the Swedish Hans Gunnar Liljenwall, for alcohol consumption, prohibited in the modern pentathlon. In football they also debuted the yellow and red cards and the availability of substitutions for a team.

But this grand procession of world sport also had a very sour dressing: politics, which returned to affect the look of several Olympic stages. Ten days before the inauguration of the Games, a university protest gathered 50,000 people in the Plaza de Tlatelolco in the center of the city. The boys and girls tried to take advantage of the presence of the world press so that their claim was not ignored by the authorities. However, Mexican President Gustavo Díaz Ordaz gave green light to the Army to evict the area, and the bloodthirsty military opened fire on the crowd instead of using more humane methods. Human rights organisations said that about 400 people died that day and another 1000 were injured. Officially, the number is much lower. At night, firefighters cleaned the traces of the carnage with their pressure hoses, and the next day, the square dawned impeccably—as if nothing had happened there. The spokesman for the Aztec government issued a statement stating that 'tranquility is guaranteed during the Olympic Games. There is and there will be sufficient vigilance to avoid problems'.

Another incident that affected the normal development of the Games corresponded to the invasion of the capital of Czechoslovakia by the Soviet army after what was called the 'Prague Spring', which lasted from January to August 1968. The USSR and its 'Warsaw Pact' allies sent hundreds of tanks and thousands of soldiers to crush an attempt to cut the umbilical cord attached to the Kremlin. The red army repressed the rebellion in a hail of bullets and the incident concluded with 70 dead and about 300 wounded.

The political headache did not end there. On 16 October, in this case, already during the Games, African-American sprinters Tommie Smith and John Carlos, first and third respectively in the final of the 200 meters, climbed onto the podium without trainers and dressed completely in black. When the American anthem was played, they raised a fist closed wrapped in a black glove, symbol of unity of the 'Black Power'. Smith and Carlos protested in this way for the inequality this minority was suffering in those years in the United States, and for the murder of minister Martin Luther King that occurred a few months earlier. The gesture of the two athletes, who led a request adhered by several athletes, went around the world and caused horror to Brundage, who ordered the expulsion of the two sprinters from the Games. However, the head of the IOC, who had been responsible for the North American delegation in Berlin 1936 and had not expressed any objection to the Nazi salute repeated by each of the German athletes who took the podium, described the gesture of his countrymen as 'a deliberate and violent violation of the fundamental principles of the Olympic spirit'. Smith and Carlos left the Olympic Village, but their message had already been heard by the world. In Moscow, for example, the poet Yevgeny Yevtushenko wrote a ballad to honour the African-Americans.

The two sprinters had planned to run the final with their fingerless black gloves, but Carlos had forgotten his in the Olympic Village. The idea of using them in the awards ceremony was from the Australian Peter Norman—winner of silver medal in that race—who suggested that Carlos use Smith's left glove. For this reason, the images show him raising the wrong hand and not the right one. For having sympathised with the Americans, Norman was banned by his country's Olympic authorities and was not allowed to compete in Munich 1972, the following edition, despite having won his races in the qualifiers. The Australian sprinter died in 2006, and Smith and Carlos traveled to Australia especially to participate in the funeral of his friend and be two of the bearers of his coffin.

Two days after the resounding case, on 18 October, the three medalists of the 400 meters, all African-Americans—Lee Evans, Larry James and Ron Freeman—climbed the podium with black berets and also raised their fists, although without gloves when the anthem of the country was sung. Evans had planned not to participate in the final in solidarity with Smith and Carlos, but the other two convinced him to run and win. In the midst of the scandal, a journalist interviewed the legendary runner James 'Jesse' Owens, hero of the Berlin Games, in the United States. 'These kids are imbued with the idea that there's a great deal of injustice in our nation. In their own way, they were trying to bring out what is wrong in our country,' he said. But he emphasised: 'This was the wrong battlefield. Their running performances would have done more to alleviate the problem rather than the disrespect they showed to our flag and the discourtesy shown to the Mexican Government'. But the great sprinter added in another interview to a group of journalists: 'You are white and cannot know what we feel. When you are hungry and wish to eat, you have never been told in a restaurant that you could not be admitted. You never suffered with your wives, on a vacation, that a hotel would deny you a room, with many available, because blacks were not allowed there. You cannot know, you cannot understand if you are not black'.

SEX VERIFICATION

In Mexico 1968, the IOC decided to include the 'sex test' for all athletes, after suspicions raised in other editions with some female participants, who exhibited remarkable feats, similar to that of contemporary male. According to the Catalan newspaper *La Vanguardia*, 'all athletes have voluntarily passed the sex exam. The problem that arose with the International Swimming Federation, in wich there was some opposition to this test, has been completely resolved, thanks to the cooperation of all athletes'.

THE END OF ABEBE

The Ethiopian legend Abebe Bikila failed in the only marathon in which he was the top candidate for gold. After his barefoot triumph in Rome 1960 and his victory in Tokyo 1964 (six weeks after being operated on the appendix), the relentless run of Bikila was crushed. On his way back to his country, the two-time champion suffered a terrible road accident in the capital while driving the Volkswagen Beetle that Emperor Haile Selassie had given him for his sporting successes. Bikila, who had been paralysed, was especially invited to the 1972 Munich Games. Upon returning to Ethiopia, the former athlete's health worsened. Abebe died on 23 October 1973 because of a stroke. More than 75,000 people attended his funeral and Emperor Selassie decreed a mourning day for the death of the national hero.

A LITTLE CASUALNESS COSTS MUCH

Argentine swimmer Luis Nicolao was a favourite to win gold in the 100-meter butterfly contest because he had broken the previous world record twice in 1962. On the morning of 20 October, the South American won with a good time in the seventh series of the first round and qualified for the semi-finals, scheduled for the afternoon in the Olympic pool Francisco Márquez Complex. Nicolao returned to the Olympic Village to have his lunch and rest until the time to jump into the water again. However, the Argentine did not show up for the second round and was eliminated. What happened? After the rest, Nicolao got on the official bus that made the transfers from the Olympic Village to the different stadiums. What the swimmer ignored, despite the driver's warning, was that the marathon was being carried out at that time, and vehicular traffic was prohibited from several streets of the city. The bus was caught more than two hours between security fences and a long line of cars, whose drivers had not taken the precaution of looking for an alternative route. For Nicolao, continuing on foot would have been useless, since that street was fenced and the foot cross was prohibited. In addition, the pool was far away. Although other swimmers, judges and assistants were traveling at that moment with the Southamerican athlete, the semi-finals were held anyway at the agreed time. The Argentine and his desire to get a medal drowned in a sea of cars.

OVERCOMING

On 13 October, the Kenyan Kipchoge 'Kip' Keino had to abandon the 10,000-meter race. Well trained and adapted to the height of Mexico, the African ran into an unexpected infection in the gallbladder that, less than a kilometer from the finishing line, began to cause an unbearable acute stitch at the stomach. Keino was transferred to a medical service, where a doctor advised him to leave the Games after reviewing him. The professional warned the athlete that if he returned to the track, he was at risk of dying in the middle of the contest. However, the Kenyan ignored the doctor's advice and a week later participated in the 5000 meters. Although the pain continued, he reached the goal just a tenth of a second behind the champion, the Moroccan Mohamad Gammoudi, and won the silver medal. Three days later, still annoyed by the infection, Keino was going by bus to the National Stadium to intervene in the 1500-meter final and his vehicle was trapped in the same traffic jam that harmed Argentine swimmer Luis Nicolao. Far from surrendering, Kip got off the bus and ran the 3 kilometers that separated him from the Colosseum. The African entered the track when there were only a few seconds left for the start of the race, but with a boost that allowed him to win the gold medal with a new Olympic record.

Overcome the malaise, the Kenyan returned to the Games in the next edition, where he had to settle for silver in the 1500 meters, but seized another gold in the 3000-meter steeplechase race. Withdrew from athletics, Keino set up a farm in his country to accommodate orphan children.

MUNICH 1972

The best four words to suffice the Olympic 1972 are 'difficult and terrible events'. The early morning of 5 September—nine days after the opening of the event—eight Palestinian members of the radical organisation 'Black September' sneaked into the Olympic Village with guns and grenades, killed two Israeli athletes and took nine others as hostages. Ironically, the terrorists had been helped to climb the walls of the property by the athletes of the American team, who seeing them dressed in sports costums, believed that they were participants who returned after a night of revelry like them. Another unusual fact was that the Palestinians had confused rooms and first assaulted one of the Uruguayan delegation, neighbour of the Israelites. Realising their mistake, the intruders turned to the place of the Hebrews without hurting the Orientals.

Seconds after the extremists captured the Jews, the Olympic Village was surrounded by police, alerted by athletes and volunteers who had noticed what was happening. In their first contact with the negotiators of the security force, the terrorists demanded the release of 234 of their fellow prisoners in Israeli prisons and their transfer to Egypt. But the Prime Minister of the Hebrew state, Golda Meir, was forceful: 'We don't negotiate with terrorists'. After several hours of tension and arduous conversations, in which there were also delegates from Arab countries who offered as intermediaries, the Palestinians managed to fly in two helicopters with their prisoners to the Fürstenfeldbruck air base, where a Lufthansa Boeing 727 aircraft was waited for them to escape to the Middle East. However, it was only a staging. The authorities had drawn up a complex rescue plan with snipers and agents disguised as pilots. Upon being received at the air station by a shower of bullets, the extremists executed all the hostages. Five terrorists were killed by snipers, three were captured and a German police officer joined the terrible list when he was shot by one of the terrorists. Perhaps the most incredible thing about this case is that, after so much blood from the most chilling attack in a sports tournament, the Olympiad was only suspended for one day, on 5 September. Brundage and other members of the IOC indicated that the attack could not affect the celebration of the Games in any way. On 6 September in the morning, a tribute to the victims was observed at the Olympiastadion, which was accompanied by 80,000 spectators and 3000 athletes. Brundage, with total lack of tact, did not even mention the Israelites killed during his speech. Spanish journalist Francisco Yagüe said in his book, *History of the Olympics* that '...after all, the Jewish death camp in Dachau was only 30 kilometers from the stadium'. The Olympic flag was hoisted at half mast as a sign of mourning along with most of the national standards of the participating countries, except those of the Arab nations: they demanded that their colours fly on top of the mast, so as not to give in to Israel. The first competition with which in the afternoon the Games continued, was the lifting of weights, precisely the contest in which three of the murdered Hebrews were supposed to participate.The Israeli delegation, which had nine survivors that had managed to escape the terrorists, withdrew from Munich. The remaining competitions were held with incompressible enthusiasm, as if nothing had happened.

SPITZ

The great sports landmark of Munich was overshadowed by the terrible terrorist attack. The American swimmer Mark Spitz reached a performance that, until that moment, seemed impossible: to win 7 gold medals in a single Game, all with world records. Spitz, who had already harvested golds twice, a silver and a bronze in Mexico 1968, won the 100- and 200-meter freestyle, the 4x100 and 4x200 freestyle relays, the 100- and 200-meter butterfly and the 4x100 medley relay. The fabulous swimmer's performance was only surpassed thirty-six years later in Beijing 2008 by his compatriot Michael Phelps.

However, as a matter of fact, Spitz was about to lose all his medals for having posed on the edge of the Olympic pool before reporters around the world with a pair of Adidas shoes in his hands. The champion had climbed the podium in sneakers but when he descended he took off those and greeted the spectators with the Adidas in his hands facing the cameras. The obvious marketing move was denounced by the Soviet team, based on the rules of amateur sport and the prohibition that, at that time, the IOC imposed on athletes to promote any sports product. However, the organisation acted with softness and in a very different way than that of the cases of the Finnish Paavo Nurmi or the American Jim Torphe, and after a brief investigation, the multiple medalist was absolved. According to the IOC, Spitz had had a 'naive' gesture, his shoes 'were old' and had not received any payment from Adidas in exchange for displaying them. Yes, of course...

SAME JOURNEY, DIFFERENT DESTINATIONS

At noon on 31 August, American sprinters, Reynaud Robinson, Edward Hart and Robert Taylor returned to the Olympic Village satisfied. That morning, the three had won their respective series (sixth, eleventh and twelfth) of the first round in the 100 meters and according to the schedule that had been informed by their coach, Stan Wright, they could rest until 7 pm in the afternoon, the time scheduled for the quarter-final races. After a restful nap, Robinson turned on the television in the room minutes after 4 pm and almost fainted: the images that came live from the stadium showed a group of athletes preparing to participate in the next round of the hectometer. Noting that the schedule that Wright had informed them was incorrect, Hart, Taylor and Robinson ran to the track, located a mile from the villa. Upon arriving at the Colosseum, Robinson and Hart were greeted with bad news: the qualifiers 1 and 2, for which they had registered, had already been made. The one who did arrive on time was Taylor, who still had a handful of seconds left for his race. Without heating, for the shot towards the stadium, Taylor was second in the test, behind an amazing Ukrainian sprinter Valeri Borzov, and went to the semi-final the next day. Coincidentally, Borzov and Taylor would repeat in the same order 1 and 2 in the final. Hart was able to sweeten his annoyance with a gold medal in the 4x100 relay, in which he was accompanied by Taylor. Robinson, on the other hand, was not chosen and returned home without any medal.

BOWLED FOR BOWEL

Having won the bronze medal in the 10,000 meters, on 3 September, the Ethiopian runner, Miruts Yifter, had to participate four days later in the preliminary 5000-meter race. However, the African did not appear that morning on the track of Olympiastadion. Officially, a leader of the Ethiopian delegation briefly stated that Yifter was ill. What the spokesperson did not specify was that the athlete did not show up at the stadium because he could not detach himself from the toilet in his room. Affected by a tremendous diarrhea, the twenty-eight-year-old athlete spent half the day in the bathroom, and the other half in his bed, exhausted. Yifter swore that he would have his revenge four years later, in Montreal. But his dreams went with the toilet flush when politics interfered in the sports and most of the states of the 'Black Continent' (Ethiopia among them) staged a boycott of the Games against apartheid in South Africa, whose white government segregated the black majority. For Moscow 1980, the runner traveled at the age of thirty-six, and presumably, with few possibilities. On the track, with more force than ever, Yifter evacuated all doubts by deploying a great performance that allowed him to chain two wins, in the 5000 and the 10,000 meters, and won two gold medals.

END OF AN UNDEFEATED STREAK

The powerful US basketball team went to Munich with an immaculate triumphant series of fifty-five victories in seven Games. The Yankee squad had never lost in an Olympiad since this sport had been included in Berlin 1936. The winning streak continued with seven victories in the initial round (against Cuba, Brazil, Czechoslovakia, Spain, Australia, Japan and Egypt) and in the semi-final with Italy. On 9 September, facing the Soviet Union, the United States met a hard rival. The duel was as hot as even. Three seconds from the end, with the score 49–48 for the Soviets, the American Doug Collins received a foul from Sako Sakandelidze, which allowed him to turn the score. The Europeans made a fast move, but their final attack was fruitless and the Americans began a crazy party to celebrate the most difficult gold medal in eight Olympic editions. However, at the control table, the game was not over. The red coach, Vladimir Kondrashin, yelled at the judges and the International Basketball Federation (FIBA) delegates that he had asked for 'time' after Collins' second conversion, and that Italian referee Renato Righetto had ignored him. The strong discussion included technicians and assistants from both squads and lasted several minutes until it was settled by the General Secretary of the FIBA, the

British William Jones, who validated the complaint of Kondrashin and ordered the three seconds to be played again. Rabid, the Americans returned to the court 'protesting'. After the restart whistle of the match, Iván Yedeshko threw a perfect pass to Aleksandr Belov, who slipped between Tom McMillen and Kevin Joyce and overturned the double winner at the edge of the final ring. End of the game and end of the undefeated streak. While the Soviets hugged each other happily for their miracle, the defeated players went directly to the Olympic Village, without accepting their silver medals. The awards ceremony was held only with the staffs of the Soviet Union and Cuba (winners of bronze after beating Italy), and the second step of the empty podium. One of the American basketball players, Kenneth Davis, wrote in his will that, after his death, no member of his family can accept the unhappy present. Thirty years after the controversial meeting, the British Jones said his decision had been correct, but acknowledged that, because it was an Olympic tournament, he had no authority to order that step. Just in case, he never set foot in the United States again.

GOOD EYE

The head of the 'Lost and Found' Office of the Olympic Village was frozen. The woman was used to receive handbags, photo cameras, perfumes, cigarette packs, T-shirts, slippers, even a wallet of a Polish athlete with 645 cash marks inside. But what she saw on her desk puzzled her. How could someone have forgotten a glass eye in one's room? The crystal ball, with its green pupil, had been left by its owner in one of the rooms of the sport neighbourhood, where it was found by a cleaning worker. 'There is a new winner,' the woman thought. She placed the sphere in a little box, the strangest of the 2763 personal things left by athletes and coaches, and put it next to the second most amazing thing left out: a seven-piece denture.

MONTREAL 1976

Although no game was played and it had been off the Olympic calendar for fifty-two years, rugby was a crucial sport in the development of the Montreal Games. In early 1976, the New Zealand rugby team, 'All Blacks', played a friendly match against the South African 'Springboks', despite the fact that all sports teams in that country of Africa were banned from all international activities because of apartheid imposed by the white minority that ruled the nation. The New Zealand insolence caused horror to most of the 'Black Continent' countries, which demanded that the IOC not allow the state of Oceania to participate in the Games. After being analysed by the committee, the claim was dismissed. Especially since a few weeks before the start of the Olympiad, another South African team, in this case of cricket, had intervened in a friendly…in Montreal! If the protest had been accepted, the participation of Canada, the host country, should also have been vetoed. As a result of the IOC ruling, twenty-five African countries refused to travel to North America. And naturally, it became the biggest Olympic boycott in history.

In the field of sports, the Soviet Union won again in the general table, with 125 medals (49 golds), over the United States, which added 94 (34 golds).

The Olympic flame experienced two unusual events: first, the traditional torch was lit by satellite signal from Athens, four days before the start of the Games, on 17 July. The fire traveled from Olympia to the Greek capital and from there, complex high-tech devices transformed it into 'ionic particles' that, by telephone signals, were transferred to Ottawa. Once the torch was lit, the relay was deployed for 230 kilometers to the stadium in the city of Montreal, the most important city in the Francophone province of Quebec. The second incident took place almost at the end of the sporting event: because of a great storm, the Olympic flame was extinguished. The problem was remedied within a few minutes by an employee, who used his own cigarette lighter, in an episode that had hardly anything sacred.

During the opening ceremony, larks were released for the first time instead of traditional pigeons, symbols of peace, since larks represent 'love and freedom' for Canadians.

MONEY MATTERS

There happened a very unfortunate event for the Uruguyan national football team. After having achieved the second place in the pre-Olympic championship played in the Brazilian city of Recife, the light blue squad—undefeated and with two gold medals—had the possibility of competing again in the Games after forty-eight years. However, the team could not travel to Montreal because it did not have enough financial means. Uruguay only sent nine athletes to Canada (five cyclists, a boxer, a rower, a swimmer and a pentathlete) who had weak performances and did not get any medal.

EMERGENCY PODIUMS

Hours before the start of the opening ceremony, the organisers almost fainted: all the podiums that had been commissioned from a local carpenter were poorly done. The craftsman had erroneously taken the measurements of the plans and had built the platforms too high. The carpenter had to hit the saw all night hard to mend his mistake and finish his work in time.

COMANECI

The star of the Games was a fourteen-year-old Romanian girl named Nadia Comaneci. The teenager not only reaped three golds, a silver and a bronze, but also became the first gymnast to obtain the score of 10 points in an Olympiad, and not only in one discipline, but in two! Her perfect performances were on the asymmetrical bars and on the balance beam. In Moscow 1980, Comaneci added two golds and two silvers to a brillant campaign of nine medals in two Olympic editions. In 1989, the champion escaped from Romania—at that time, under the political command of the Soviet Union, which prompted many people to flee for political reasons—and settled in the United States, where she was a model of underwear, lingerie, equipment sports and even wedding dresses. After marrying the American gymnast Bart Conner (winner of two golds at the 1984 Los Angeles Games), Comaneci worked as a promoter of physical activity, attended an academy inaugurated with her husband and was a television commentator on the Games and gymnastics championships.

BATTERY-POWERED SWORD

The performance of the Soviet Union in the modern pentathlon was very weak, and the podium was moving away in each event. Their last hope was that the best swordsman of the team, Boris Grigoryevich Onishchenko, who, they wished, would repeat his brilliant performance from Munich, which earned him an individual silver and gold for the team. On his first duel, Onishchenko faced British captain Jim Fox, who he easily defeated with just one touch. But Fox strongly protested the result: he claimed that his opponent's sword had never touched him. The judges did not understand the British's claim. Although the maneuver had been very quick in the eyes of the spectators, it was clear that the Soviet's weapon had reached its target, because it had sounded the alarm and turned on the coloured light. Fox's conviction aroused the curiosity of the test director, who ordered the confiscation of Onishchenko's weapon. Upon checking the sword, the referee discovered that the hilt included a switch and a battery that generated an electric shock that, despite failing to reach the opponent's chest, operated its sensors. The Soviet cheater was immediately disqualified, both from the individual and the collective contest, which unleashed the hatred of his companions who were not aware of the vile maneuver. Onishchenko had to even leave the Olympic Village, because volleyball players from his own country threatened to throw him out of the window of the building, offended by the scandal that had affected the entire red delegation.

EXPENSIVE STRENGTH

The Russian national, Vasili Ivanovich Alekseyev, is considered the best weightlifter in history. The strong man born in Pokrovo-Shishkino, who in Montreal won his second consecutive Olympic gold medal, broke 80 world records between 1970 and 1978. He was the first man to lift more than 227 kilos in the clean and jerk competition and break the barrier of the 600 kilos in the triple event of press, snatch and jerk. Almost 1.85 meters tall and about 160 kilograms in weight, Alekseyev proclaimed himself an enemy of steroids and other prohibited drugs. 'I know stimulants, but they are harmful to health. I do sports because I love it and I don't like to punish the body with harmful substances,' he said. His secret lay in a peculiar diet designed by himself and kept absolutely secret until his retirement, after the 1980 Moscow Games, which allowed him to develop a huge power. The regime included the intake of 500 grams of premium Russian caviar per day, a delicacy as nutritious as it is highly expensive outside Russia. According to the prices of duty-free shops in the airports of Western Europe and America—much lower than those of the stores in the cities—the weightlifter swallowed caviar for an equivalent of about 800 USD a day. Of course, Alekseyev bought this delicacy in the local market, where the amount was less than 10 per cent.

WATER AND FIRE

The British nationals, David Hunt and Alan Warren, showed up at the Portsmouth Olympic Port, on the edge of Lake Ontario, as serious podium candidates in the Tempest class. Hunt and Warren had enough scrolls to claim a medal, after the silver they had won four years earlier in the German city of Kiel, where the races of the Munich Games were held. However, their performance in Canada was disastrous. On 27 July, after a week of competition, the British finished fourteenth out of sixteenth participants, just ahead of Puerto Rico and the Philippines. Very angry with the result, Hunt and Warren unloaded their fury against their poor boat, which they sprayed with fuel and set fire.

MEDIEVAL GLORY

The Japanese gymnast Shun Fujimoto miscalculated his final jump in the floor exercise and fell on the mat of the Montreal Forum. When he tried to get up, an intense prick in his right knee turned him back. The agonising gesture of the athlete worried the managers of the Japanese team, who requested the immediate assistance of a doctor. When checking the injured in the locker room, the doctor discovered that the Japanese had broken ligaments. 'I'm sorry, boy, but you should leave the competition,' said the specialist. But Fujimoto, owner of an unusual fortitude, refused to give up the Games and leave his teammates. The brave man decided to intervene in the two remaining contests, pommel horse and rings, despite the fact that the injury, in addition to causing great pain, could be aggravated with the jumps that one is supposed to do at the end of each of the exercises. Armed with great courage, Fujimoto, who had hidden the injury to his teammates and also to his coach, climbed the easel, and after developing his routine almost flawlessly, landed with his feet together, as if nothing happened to him. The jury rated him with a positive score of 9.5, but inside, the condition had even deteriorated: the jump had aggravated the damage. The doctor rechecked the Japanese and warned him that, if he fell badly from the rings, located almost 3 meters from the ground, the injury could cause him a permanent disability. Fujimoto hung on the rings to complete his task. His routine came out as he had rehearsed before the accident, and falling on the mat, he managed to keep his balance and raise his arms; the judges awarded him 9.7 points. The gymnast ended up overwhelmed by the suffering, although very proud to have contributed so that Japan remained with the gold medal after defeating, by a narrow margin, the Soviet Union team. Several years later, he revealed in an interview that the damage was irreparable for his medial, anterior and posterior cruciate ligaments. 'Even today, if I try to stand up, my knee sometimes pops out,' said the heroic samurai.

MOSCOW 1980

Moscow 1980 hosted the biggest Olympic boycott in history. The United States promoted a massive rejection based on the Soviet invasion in Afghanistan, which took place in December 1979. US President James 'Jimmy' Carter considered that 'going to Moscow would be a seal of approval for the foreign policy of the Soviet Union', and sixty-four nations—mostly from America, Africa and Asia—joined the initiative. In Europe, only Norway and the Federal Republic of Germany officially participated in the boycott, while athletes from countries that were historically allies of the United States, such as Great Britain or France, came despite the decision of their governments and performed under the Olympic flag of their respective states. Similarly, every time an athlete or team from any of these countries won a gold, instead of the corresponding national anthem, the representative song of the IOC was played.

Only eighty nations attended Moscow—the smallest number since Melbourne 1956—which significantly reduced the quality of the event. This situation disrupted the organisation's chart of most sports, for which Western athletes and teams had mostly classified. In some competitions, such as field hockey, the host squad was the only partcipant; so it was necessary to resort to last-minute invitations to nations with lower-quality teams to carry out the tournament. Representatives of several of the nations that had joined the boycott urged the IOC to cancel the Games, but the head of the organisation, the Irishman Michael Morris, said that 'only a third world war can prevent it'. Killanin accused the US president of being 'an incompetent' and not having 'any notion of what sport is. If baseball or American football had been Olympic sports, Carter would not have triggered the boycott of Moscow 1980. I hope that, in the future, the heads of state will be better informed of what sport is, what *Olympism* means and the transcendental influence that both have on the formation of tomorrow's society'.

Without the US opposition, the Soviet team won easily in the general table, with 195 medals (80 golds), followed by the German Democratic Republic, with 126 (47 golds).

The Olympiad closed with another Yankee statement. The Washington government managed to prevent the IOC from raising the American flag at the closing ceremony on 3 August. As the protocol demanded, the presence of the host state of the next edition, the colourful banner of the city of Los Angeles was raised.

IS THAT JIMMY CARTER AT THE GAMES?

Eastern European press highlighted a funny coincidence: Jimmy Carter ordered the boycott against the Moscow Games but Jimmy Carter competed in the Olympiad. The US president James Earl 'Jimmy' Carter had a homonym—the Scottish James Hill 'Jimmy' Carter, who intervened in the swimming competition. The British, who had passed through Munich and Montreal without success, also did not stand out in the Moscow pool, since he failed to qualify for the finals in the 200-meter backstroke. The Scot did deserve a gold medal though in the restaurant of the Olympic Village, as a prize for the highest consumption of beer. Then, completely drunk, he began a fight with the other compatriot, Gary Abraham, against other athletes, culminating in several broken tables and chairs. Carter was expelled from the Games by the British managers. The drunken scandal generated even more jokes in the communist press, which wondered slyly if both 'Jimmy' had something else in common, apart from the name.

THE BOXER WHO LOST THE SAME FIGHT TWICE

The title of this story suggests a situation that is ideally impossible. But the history of the Olympic Games, as this book tells, shows that in a sports competition everything can happen. In this case, the protagonist is the bantamweight figther Moussa Sangare, from Mali. Sangare, the only boxer who represented his country in Moscow, was disqualified on 19 July for not appearing in time for official weighing in the Olimpiyskiy, the covered stadium where the tournament took place. However, this sanction was reversed after Mali delegates explained that the delay was not the responsibility of the fighter, but of the plane that had transported him, which had suffered an extensive delay on one of the stopovers before landing in the Soviet capital. The judges knew that the championships were already decimated enough by the Western boycott to become extremely strict with 'little things'. Rehabilitated, Sangare climbed into the ring on 20 July to face Zambio Lucky Mutale. If he had known that he was going to suffer a tremendous beating, the Mali international not only did appeal for his disqualification, but directly refused to get on the plane that took him to Moscow.

LUCKY FRACTURE

Two days before participating in the shooting contest at the Dynamo club in the Moscow neighbourhood of Mytishchi, Hungarian national Károly Varga suffered a severe blow to his right hand while playing soccer, that caused a bone fracture. Varga was treated by a doctor who immobilised the limb, although he released his fingers so that he could intervene in the small-bore rifle contest lying on the ground. When trying to grip his weapon, the Hungarian discovered that, if he gently pulled the trigger, the injury did not hurt so much and, at the same time, his pulse was firmer. On 21 July, *helped* by the pain generated by the wound, Varga improved his performance and won the gold medal with a world record. The fracture had given him a hand.

A DEADLY INJURY

On 26 July, the Soviet Union and Poland faced each other in the semi-final of the team fencing tournament, foil category. The young Belarusian Vladimir Lapitsky (who had fallen in his duels with Marian Sypniewski and Lech Koziejowski, but had surpassed Boguslaw Zych) defeated Adam Robak 2–1. In the fourth set, the Polish attacked thoroughly: his weapon eluded Lapitsky's defense and stuck in the left sector of his chest after destroying the protective vest. Although he suffered a significant loss of blood due to the rupture of a vein, the Soviet considered himself lucky because the tip of the sword passed millimeters away from his heart, which would have caused an immediate death. From his bed in the hospital, Lapitsky received another good news: his team had surpassed Poland and had won the silver medal.

AN UNDUE ADVANTAGE?

The judges looked once, twice, thrice the photos of the final of the female 100-meter held on 26 July at the Lenin Stadium and could not determine who had been the champion. The timers had marked a draw in 11.06 seconds between the two fastest, the Soviet national, Lyudmila Kondratyeva and the Eastern German national, Marlies Oelsner-Göhr, so that the images were the only way out of the thorny problem. After observing every detail of the photographs, the judges noticed that the heads of the Soviet and the German had crossed the finishing line aligned, as well as their shoulders, hips and legs. However, unanimously, they decided that the winner had been Kondratyeva, for a 'little' anatomical advantage: her breasts were more bulky than those of her rival.

REPUDIATED MEDAL

On 1 August, the Soviet football team defeated the Yugoslavian by 2–0, with goals from Khoren Oganesian and Sergei Andreyev, both in the second half, and took the bronze medal. While the local players celebrated the victory, from the stands began to rain boos from the few spectators present at the Dynamo club stadium. The fans were furious with their team, which had started the Olympic campaign with bulky scores like an 8-0 to Cuba, in the group stage, but later the red march had blurred. The USSR needed the help of the Mexican referee, Mario Rubio Vázquez, to eliminate the weak team of Kuwait by 2–1 in the quarter-finals. In the next round, the host squad fell 1–0 against the German Democratic Republic which in the culminating match would be overtaken by Czechoslovakia in 1–0. The defeat, which shattered the golden dreams, infiurated fans so much that the game for third place, initially scheduled at the Lenin stadium with a capacity for 90,000 spectators, moved to a smaller setting with 35,000 people. But the new coloseum was giant anyway, like the failure of the local team.

SURPRISE

One of the tournaments most affected by the Western boycott was women's field hockey, which made its debut as an Olympic sport in the Soviet Olympiad. Five of the six classified countries had joined the mass desertion. The exception was the local team. To overcome the problem that threatened the very existence of the championship, the organisers were forced to invite nations with very little or no experience in this discipline, such as Austria or Poland. Another summoned, Czechoslovakia, had at least participated in the 1978 World Championship, although without success. From Africa, Zimbabwe was presented, a country that had just become independent from the United Kingdom. Until then, its name was Rhodesia and it had been expelled from the IOC and banned to intervene in Munich 1972 and Montreal 1976 because its government supported the political segregationism.

Without games beyond its borders, fifteen Zimbabweans of very white skin and English ancestry was the surprise winner of the tournament. With three victories (4–0 to Poland, 2–0 to the USSR and 4–1 to Austria) and two draws (with Czechoslovakia and India), the African girls gave their young nation the first gold medal of its history.

LOS ANGELES 1984

Los Angeles 1984 is usually remembered for the revenge boycott of the Soviet bloc. However, the twenty-third edition of the Games (in fact, the twentieth edition, if the three 'ghost' tournaments suspended by the First and Second World War are discounted) was key to the path-breaking development that the modern Olympics have been carrying along. From the hand of the new president of the IOC, the Spaniard Juan Antonio Samaranch, in California began the process that, eight years later, would decree the death of amateurism. This Catalan owner of an exceptional instinct for business was the pillar that finished breaking down the precepts that almost a century earlier had tried to set on fire Pierre de Coubertin. The passage of time and the advancement of communications, marketing and advertising erased the debatable commandments that prohibited professionalism. Much can be questioned about the excessive intrusion of companies in the world of sports, but their role is undoubtedly less harmful to their development than an elitist doctrine called 'amateurism'. Without the support of the State (admitted and not disguised as public employment, as in the communist countries during the second half of the 20th century) or of the 'sponsors', a poor athlete must take time away from training and rest to devote to a job that supports his way of life. An athlete born into a rich family does not need to invest in a work occupation and can dedicate himself exclusively to practices and repose.

These Games were the first to be organised by a private entity without State participation, and also, by chance, the first that did not generate losses but large profits, estimated at about 150 million USD. Each event of the Olympiad was scheduled to raise money, until the extensive race of the Olympic torch. With a vision perhaps 'hyper-commercial', the organisers decided to rent the post of the sacred flame at a rate of about 3000 USD a kilometer. Several opulent businessmen signed up for the event to feel themselves as elite athletes at least for a moment. Not all of the extensive route—about 15,000 kilometers through thirty-three American states—was rented, but it did collect several million USD.

This edition is also recognised as the first 'battlefield' that violently confronted sports product companies. After several years of hegemony of Adidas and Puma, the two German brands discovered that there were two new rivals on the court: Nike and Reebok.

The boycott promoted by the Soviet Union, a revanchist demonstration for what happened four years earlier in Moscow, had a much lower weight than in 1980: only fourteen countries adhered, mostly satellites of the communist government of the Kremlin. The absence of the eastern states gave an exaggerated advantage to the local team to obtain a large victory with 174 medals (83 golds), followed very far by West Germany with 59 medals (only 17 golds).

The Libyan sports delegation withdrew from the Olympics after three alleged journalists from that African country were denied entry to the United States. The US State Department said the three men had 'nothing to do' with any newspaper, radio or other media, and that it was suspected that, in reality, they were terrorists. The IOC did not give great importance to this setback. The Libyan team was made up of six athletes, of which five were members of the equestrian team.

Athletes underwent a radical change with the incorporation of the women's marathon, which was won by the American Joan Benoit.

In football, for the first time the participation of professional soccer players was allowed, although under twenty-three years of age and without a background in World Cups (something that would later be reversed by enabling three 'seniors' per team). After eight tournaments won by the 'communist' countries—which supposedly used amateur players disguised as State employees although in international category 'A' games—France was left with the gold after defeating Brazil in the final by 2–0 at the Rose Bowl stadium in Pasadena, California.

KOREAN STEW

The yellow smoke that densely emerged under the door of one of the rooms of the Korean delegation scared the volunteer. The Californian, perhaps experienced by so many forest fires that plague the state every summer, knew about the dangers of the flames and ran to give notice to the firemen, afraid that the fire would spread throughout the Olympic Village. A crew arrived at the place in a few seconds, and upon entering the room, discovered with surprise that the smoke did not correspond to an igneous focus, but to a saucepan where a hungry group of oriental athletes stewed a fat snake. 'In the restaurant of the Village they don't prepare this delicacy for us,' the Oriental athletes justified. Catched with their hands in the thick broth, the yellow athletes swore by their mothers that the snake intake had a double value: on one hand, that stew, strange handle for Westerners, was very healthy and provided the necessary nutrients for the competition; on the other, it worked like an elixir to fight the melancholy produced for staying so many days away from home. Friendly, the Koreans offered their exotic dish, but the agents, perhaps frightened by the smell that came from the cauldron, politely declined the treat and chose to get away from the place 'faster than a fireman'.

IN THE NAME OF THE SISTER

Puerto Rican athlete Madeline de Jesús could not overcome the long jump qualifying stage held on 8 August. A muscular discomfort prevented her from displaying her full potential. To make matters worse, the injury was aggravated with the successive leaps, so that the young woman was unable to participate in the other contest in which she was enrolled, the 4x400 relay. In order to not harm her race partners, Madeline met that afternoon with her twin sister Margaret, who had traveled to Los Angeles to witness the Games as a spectator, and asked her to impersonate her in the team relay that would take place in two more days. Margaret, who also practised athletic disciplines but not at the level of her sister, accepted, but on condition that the trick was a fierce secret between them. Not even coach Francisco Colón Alers or the relay partners—Evelyn and Marie Mathieu and Angelita Lind—should know. Madeline agreed and accepted, confident that she and her sister were almost two drops of water. They even cut and combed their hair the same way. On 10 August, on the track of the Memorial Coliseum, Puerto Rico showed up for the first tie with the United States, Great Britain, Jamaica and India with three 'regular' runners and an imposter, who wore the official uniform and the number of her twin. With Margaret instead of Madeline, the Caribbean team was in the last place of its group, but qualified for the final because it achieved a better time than Antigua and Ghana in the second series.

At the end of the race, a Puerto Rican journalist, Luis Varela, who was working for the American news agency Associated Press (AP) and knew the De Jesús sisters very well, discovered that the girl who had intervened was not Madeline but her twin. How? Because Margaret had a small mole on her face that her sister didn't have. This detail went unnoticed by most people, except for those who were familiar with the girls. Varela asked Colon Alers why he had allowed the participation of a sprinter who was not enrolled in the Olympiad. The coach almost fainted. When he discovered what was happening, Colon Alers, very angry at the fraud of which he had been a victim, reported the case to the president of the Olympic Committee of his country, Germán Rieckehoff Sampayo, who demanded that his team be removed from the finals of the following day. Rieckehoff Sampayo did not notify the organisers of the competition that his team had incurred a fraud with an athlete who, in order to impersonate another, had violated the security and identification controls. Upon returning to the Caribbean island, the sisters were suspended for life from official competitions.

It is said that the disgust caused by the naughty girls provoked a deep depression to the coach, who died a few months later. However, his prestige as a professional and his unusual honesty made his name transcend his physical disappearance and remained linked to Puerto Rican athletics. The main sports complex in the city of Ponce was named Francisco Colón Alers in his honour.

KILL ONE BIRD WITH TWO STONES

The Swedish Nils Martin had lost one of the moving targets of the modern pentathlon shooting contest. With a very weak performance in almost all the tests on his back, Martin waited for his next objective and, with an extra projectile, shot him twice to ensure the success. What the Swede did not take into account was that the judges warned of his trick and annulled his performance at that stage. With no points in the shooting event, Martin collapsed to the bottom of the table, to forty-seventh place among fifty-two participants. The penalty also affected the Swedish team, which went from being near the podium to the tenth place, because of the cheater. Martin's companions, Svante Rasmuson (winner of silver in the individual category) and Martin Lamprecht, agreed that his attitude had been doubly irresponsible.

THE PUNCH THAT DEFINED TWO FIGHTS

Can a single punch resolve two boxing fights? Yes, in fact it happened on 9 August at the Los Angeles Memorial Sports Arena, where a blow that entered at the wrong time for thousandths of a second, and a controversial arbitration decision resolved the light-heavyweight category tournament. The unusual situation took as a snack the beating that Yugoslav Anton Josipovic gave Algerian Mustafa Moussa in the first semi-final. Moussa, the surprise star of the competition, returned home with a bronze medal, although he had to spend a small season in the hospital first. In the second qualifying duel for the golden combat, the local idol and top candidate Evander Holyfield—who arrived with three knockouts in three previous matches—easily dominated the New Zealander, Kevin Barry. In the second round, Holyfield combined a right to the ribs with a hook to the jaw that sent Barry to sleep on the canvas. The Yugoslav referee Gligorije Novicic, instead of raising his arm as a winner to the American, disqualified him and took the lawsuit to the New Zealander, who only looked successful in dreams. Neither the spectators nor Holyfield himself could understand anything. Novicic explained that he had shouted 'stop' moments before the lethal punch came out. The American swore that he had not heard anything amid the tremendous screaming of the public. The recording, passed in slow motion, revealed that in effect the referee had ordered the interruption less than a second before and from an angle that did not allow Holyfield to see his sign, and that Barry, before being knocked out, had also launched a fist towards his rival after the order. The New Zealander would later declare that his opponent had won 'cleanly'. The United States protested the ruling, but the International Amateur Boxing Federation ratified the decision and the bronze medal for the American. The controversial judge left the Memorial Sports Arena escorted by several policemen, who prevented the fans from assaulting him for having served gold to his compatriot Josipovic on a tray. Months later, Novicic apologised and admitted that his opinion had been rushed. But, in fact, he allowed the Yugoslav athlete to be champion without fighting against Barry, because the Olympic regulation prohibits a knocked-out boxer from fighting again before twenty-eight days. During the awards ceremony, Josipovic—a student of literature—stoically endured the booing of the spectators and, at the end of the performance of his hymn, invited Holyfield to share the first step of the podium. 'I would have liked to fight Holyfield to show what I am capable of and win the medal in the ring. I am a little disappointed that the public does not understand that it is not a pride to win like that. I asked Holyfield to accompany me on the podium because I believe that these Games represent the spirit of friendship and good wishes,' said Josipovic, who never faced the American. The Yugoslavian became a sports journalist and covered several of Holyfield's professional fights, with whom he had a deep friendship. Although he was a four-time full-weight champion, the Alabama-born boxer was never able to overcome his Los Angeles setback. In an interview, he said 'It doesn't matter how many fights I have won. They always ask me what happened at the Olympic Games'.

BAD STEP

On 10 August, the track of the Los Angeles Memorial Coliseum got overflooded with controversies. The local runner Mary Decker, 'the bride of America', a model of important brands, such as the sportswear company Nike, was the favourite to win the final 3000-meter race, a contest in which she had imposed herself, next to the 1500 meters, comfortably in the World Cup last year. In that event she had won comfortably, as in the 1500 meters, in the Athletics World Cup the previous year. But an eighteen-year-old South African girl crossed her way, Zola Budd-Pieterse, who competed for Britain for the veto that fell on her country because of apartheid. Decker started leading the test but in the middle, the competition was overtaken by Budd. Upon reaching 1700 meters, the American, trying to surpass the South African by the internal lane, got tangled up with the feet of her rival and fell loudly. The image of Decker crying like a girl moved the world. With a sprained ankle, her desire to win two gold medals had vanished. The contusion did not allow her to appear in the 1500 meters, scheduled for the next day. Budd continued running bathed by the boos and insults of the public, and finished in the seventh place. Favoured by the incident, the Romanian Maricica Puica won the race with Olympic record. 'I blame her. I understand she doesn't have the experience to understand what she did. I don't think she did it intentionally but that doesn't mean she shouldn't be held responsible. They're still trying to say I was a bully and look who's paying for it. I feel like something has been stolen and the awful part is people are saying it's okay, that it's okay the way it happened,' the American complained to the press as a resentful loser. Budd was more discreet: 'I didn't see her. I didn't do anything wrong. The boos were terrible, worse than a punch in the stomach.' The secretary of the International Athletics Federation, John Holt, put an end to the controversy: 'Budd did nothing anti-regulatory, Decker was her own victim.' With Mary, another victim fell: her sponsor. According to the book *Swoosh: the Unauthorized Story of Nike*, the firm hired Decker and four other American track and field athletes who were candidates for gold for the Los Angeles Games. '(Nike) paid them the highest price and included clauses that promised them to appear in advertising,' says the text. Other competitors were promised 40,000 USD as prize money if they won the gold. These arrangements, of course, were not authorised at that time. Anyway, it was a true paradox that the main star of a shoe brand failed to entangle her feet with an African girl who, like Abebe Bikila in Rome 1960, ran barefoot.

PURE-BRED ITALIAN

Without the threatening presence of the American Mary Decker, the 1500-meter race had a surprising champion—the Italian Gabriella Dorio, a beautiful Venetian athlete who had participated without shine in Montreal and Moscow. On 11 August, Dorio surpassed two Romanians who had the best chances for winning gold according to specialists: Maricica Puica, brand new champion in the 3000 meters, and Doina Melinte, winner in the 800 meter. Puica and Melinte had to settle for silver and bronze respectively, while Dorio, pure-bred Italian, celebrated the gold medal by bathing in wine in the tub.

INDOMITABLE TRIUMPH

Carlos Alberto de Sousa Lopes could not imagine even in his wildest dream that he was going to be admitted to the Santa María hospital when he left his house on the morning of 27 July 1984, when he was training to participate in the Los Angeles Games marathon. The athlete was struck by a reckless motorist while crossing a street in Lisbon. Lopes crossed the windshield of the vehicle and ended up inside the road, hit and lacerated by the glasses on the head and legs. The thirty-seven-year-old runner was quite lucky, despite the incident: his injuries healed quickly and he was able to travel to Los Angeles to take part in the marathon, a race he had never won before and had only been able to finish once, in Rotterdam (Holland), a year before. On 12 August, sixteen days after the traffic accident and in the middle of a hot and very humid atmosphere, Lopes established himself as the most veteran champion in the history of the marathon and achieved a new Olympic record: 2 hours, 9 minutes and 21 seconds, which was just pulverised in the 2008 Beijing edition. His gold medal was also the first one obtained by a Portuguese athlete.

SEOUL 1988

Seoul 1988 was defined in 9.79 seconds and two days—9.79 seconds was the time it took Canadian sprinter Ben Johnson to finish the 100-meter race and set a new world record. Two days, which took analysts to discover that the Jamaican sprinter had used a drug called stanozolol to improve his performance. Johnson was disqualified and his gold medal went to the American, Carl Lewis. The penalty was considered 'hypocritical' by several athletes and coaches who, on the ground, claimed that Lewis's body was no cleaner than his rival's. The Johnson case was the most resonant in Olympic history because the race was held before the eyes of millions of TV viewers.

The second Oriental Games embodied, on the other hand, the last duel of the 'Cold War' on the sporting level. Two years after this Olympiad, the political and economic failure of the communist model driven by Moscow split the Union of Soviet Socialist Republics into a dozen new nations and liberated, at the same time, the 'satellite' countries located behind the curtain of iron, such as Poland, Czechoslovakia, Yugoslavia, Romania, Hungary, Bulgaria and East Germany. But in Korea, before disappearing as such from the European political map, the Soviet Union and East Germany said goodbye to the Games with a beating for the United States, which was relegated to the third place of the medal table for the first time in an olympiad (except, Moscow

1980, in which the North American country did not participate). The red team added 132 medals (55 golds), the German 102 (37 golds) and the Yankees 94 (36 golds). The United States suffered some memorable defeats, as in the men's basketball tournament, a sport in which, also for the first time, it did not reach the final. The Soviet Union won in the semi-final 82–76 and then defeated Yugoslavia in the gold game. The Yankee team had to settle for bronze.

The languor of amateurism, which already agonised, allowed tennis to return to the Olympic calendar after sixty-two years of absence. In the individual contest, the Slovak national, Miroslav Mecir (representative of Czechoslovakia) prevailed among the men, while the German, Steffi Graf did it among the women. That same year, Graf also won the Grand Slam by consecrating champion of the open of Australia, France, Great Britain and the United States, an achievement that, at the close of this edition, was not repeated either in ladies' or in gentlemen's section.

A CULINARY COMPROMISE

On the recommendation of the IOC, the Korean government ordered a ban on dishes with dogs and snakes at the restaurants in Seoul during the Games. According to an official resolution, the prohibition reached foods considered ugly by athletes, managers and Western visitors.

IRRESPONSIBLE CHAMPION

On 19 September, American Greg Louganis made a slight miscalculation while taking off from the 3-meter springboard, and when he fell into the pool, brushed the tip of the mobile platform with his head. Louganis could leave the pool by his own means, but the blow had opened a deep wound, so he had to be taken to the infirmary to have five stitches applied to his head. Recovered, the jumper, considered one of the best in history, continued with the qualifying series, and with a great performances and as if nothing had happened, went to the final round in third place. The next day, Louganis crushed his rivals and took the gold medal with great authority. A week later, the American repeated his successful routine from the 10-meter platform and added his fourth gold. Seven years later, Louganis—who had already won two golds in Los Angeles and became the only male diver in Olympic history to sweep both the diving events in consecutive Games—publicly admitted to being gay and acknowledged that he was infected with HIV. During a press conference in which he presented his autobiography, he was reminded of the accident and the spilling of a few drops of his blood in the pool. The champion admitted that he had traveled to Korea knowing that he was ill. 'It was an irresponsible decision,' the athlete acknowledged, 'because I didn't realise that it could hurt me…Imagine the most intense, pressure-filled, stressful situation you've ever been in, multiply that by ten and being under such scrutiny. Add to it an athletic event with the adrenaline flowing. It's overwhelming. It's overwhelming even if everything goes right,' he added.

Some media called on the IOC to impose blood tests on all athletes, a request that was dismissed by the organisation. Sports-illustrated magazine, which celebrated the decision, said in an editorial that Louganis 'was incomparable as an athlete. He developed his entire career with grace and dignity. He was and is loved by the American public. AIDS was spread not because he was an athlete, not because he was gay, but because he didn't practice safe sex. That's the message he should carry when he travels across the country to promote his book'.

MEDAL AND RING

German skater Christa Rothenburger liked her boyfriend and coach Ernst Luding's proposal: cycling during the summer would reinforce the work of her thighs and calves, and improve her performance on the ice. What the German had not anticipated was that the power of her legs, which had allowed her to win a couple of golds and a silver in the Winter Games, would also transport her to a podium in the Summer Olympics. At the Seoul velodrome, Rothenburger reached the final of the 1000-meter sprint contest, and on 24 September she was only three seconds away from holding the gold medal barely surpassed by the Soviet national, Erika Salumia. Christa was very close to match the golden summer–winter record of Edward Eagan, champion of boxing in Antwerp 1920 and sledding in Lake Placid in 1932, but anyway she was the first woman to win a medal in both kinds of Games. The German did not care what Eagan had done. She was so happy with her unexpected achievement that, to thank the productive suggestion, she married Luding.

SPORTING SPIRIT

The individual sailing regatta of the Finn class had a great hero, and this was not the Spanish José Luis Doreste, winner of gold medal, but the Canadian national Larry Lemieux. The North American, owner of an exquisite Olympic spirit, abandoned the race in which he fought the first place with Doreste to rescue two other participants, Singaporean internationals Chan Joseph and Siew Shaw Her. On the morning of 24 September, the ship of the Asians, who intervened in class 470, had capsized several kilometers off the coast, at the height of the city of Pusan. Lemieux, who was in the second place of the fifth Finn class race, turned to the Singaporeans who floated adrift, took them out of the water and moved them safe and sound to an official patrol boat. The Canadian considered that 'the first rule of the regattas is, if someone has problems, you help them. The first thing I thought was "Do they really need help or can they manage on their own?" I shouted asking if they were well, but I could not understand what they said. I had to go. If I went and didn't need help, "c'est la vie". But if I didn't go, I could throw it in my face for the rest of my life.' After his selfless behaviour, the Canadian returned to the competition and finished in the twenty-second place. Finishing the seven races, Lemieux was in eleventh place in the general table, quite far from the podium. 'I could have won a medal, but I did what I should do,' he said proudly. But the president of the IOC, the Spaniard Juan Antonio Samaranch, did not want the Canadian to run out of prize, and gave him something more valuable than the gold: the Pierre de Coubertin Medal for the Sports Spirit.

TWO FIGHTS, TWO RINGS, TWO KNOCKOUTS

Seoul hosted the biggest Olympic boxing tournament. A total of 432 fighters (Rio de Janeiro had 279, including female fighters who began participating in London 2012) from 106 countries competed in 12 categories. With such concurrence, the organisers had to resort to an unusual maneuver so that all the combats fit within the narrow Olympic calendar: two rings, almost stuck, were placed in the gymnasium of the Chamshil School for two simultaneous fights to be played. In an attempt to avoid auditory confusion, a bell was placed in quadrilateral 'A' to mark the beginning and end of each assault, and a siren in 'B'. This idea, which seemed positive to the IOC, caused chaos. Between the screaming of the stands and the concentration in the fight, several fights fell into unfortunate confusion. The most unusual of the disruptions occurred on 25 September, when American Todd Foster and South Korean Chun Jim Chil faced each other for the second round of the light welterweight category. The alarm rang and both contestants started the duel, accompanied by the Hungarian referee Sandor Pajar. After two thirds of the first round, neighbouring quadrilateral-bell clanked. Chil, clueless, lowered his guard convinced that his assault was over. Pajar hesitated. Foster, the only one awakened, threw a left hook that knocked down his opponent. The referee initiated the account, although upon reaching 'four' he stopped because of the strong complaints that rained from the Korean corner. Undecided, the Hungarian approached to the control table to ask what to do. There, the Bulgarian Emil Jetchev, president of the arbitration commission of the International Boxing Federation, had no answers. There was no rule that foresaw such a collapse.

After showering, Foster was sitting next to his girlfriend in the gym stalls, watching his compatriot and friend Arthur Johnson, who casually fought another South Korean, Kim Kwang Sun. An American manager approached him and informed him that the organisers had analysed his case and that he should face Chun Jim Chil again 'in 45 minutes'. The crazy decision had missed the Olympic rule that prohibits a knocked-out boxer from fighting again before twenty-eight days. Resigned, Foster returned to the ring two hours after his fight and, in the second round, knocked down the South Korean again. This time, Pajar's account ended in '10 without any mess. For the American boxer, the repetition was not free: at the end of the first round, the Korean had broken his nose with an accurate right jab. Foster had this rather uncanny honour of being the only fighter in history who defeated twice and with two knockouts to the same opponent, in a single day.

FROM THE TOILET TO THE COURT

The South American duel between Argentina and Brazil was very even. Each team had won a set in the match for the bronze medal in volleyball, played on 2 October in the gymnasium of Hanyang University, after being eliminated in the semi-finals by the Soviet Union and the United States, respectively. In the third set, Argentina won 158 and was one step away from the podium. At that significant moment, Hugo Conte, one of the best players of the light-blue and white squad, left the court and headed towards the changing rooms. 'Due to an intestinal problem I had to run to the bathroom and I missed a large part of the fourth set,' Conte explained. Sitting on the toilet, the player expected his teammates to finish off the job. But later,Conte decided that he could not stay out on the defining set and, with an enormous willpower, forgot about the persistent diarrhea and returned to the game. With his fundamental contribution, Argentina won 15–9 and took over bronze. Then, more relaxed, he returned to the toilet, but with his medal hanging from his proud chest.

BARCELONA 1992

Barcelona 1992 is considered one of the best Olympic editions in history. Far from political problems, this pearl of the Mediterranean land received all the IOC member countries without any corset. Months before the start of the competitions, representatives of the Olympic around the world agreed to erase the word 'amateurism' from the statutes and almost completely lift the barriers for professional athletes (although cyclists were left out, which would be incorporated four years later). The biggest impact of this decision was the landing of the Dream Team in Spain, a wonderful basketball team made up of famous American NBA stars. Led by Michael Jordan (considered the best player of all time), Earvin 'Magic' Johnson and Larry Bird, the American team swept all their rivals. The NBA celebrities completed the tournament with an average of 117 points per match and not only received the gold medal, but the title of best team in the history of that sport.

After the fall of the Union of Soviet Socialist Republics and the end of the 'Cold War' in 1991, the nations included in that gigantic Eurasian state presented themselves as a single block, called the 'Unified Team', with the only exception of Baltic countries: Lithuania, Latvia and Estonia. Despite the desertion of these three territories, the former reds were top in the general medal table with 112 medals(45 golds, 38 silvers and 29 bronzes) followed by the Americans with 108 medals (37 golds).

Belarusian gymnast Vitaly Shcherbo was consecrated as the great individual star of the competition, obtaining 6 gold medals, 4 of them the same day: on 2 August, at the Palau Sant Jordi, Shcherbo was consecrated in long horse vault, rings, pommel horse and parallel bars.

GAIL'S RECOVERY

The American sprinter Gail Devers was selected to compete in Seoul 1988, but she had to resign her Olympic chance affected by the rare Graves-Basedow disease, which was almost leaving her blind. Devers recovered, and on 1 August, in Barcelona got the gold medal in the 100 meters. The American could have doubled her success five days later, in the 100-meter hurdles: though leading the race, she tripped over the last obstacle and reached the finishing line in fifth place. She was one step away from matching the double that the Dutch Fanny Blankers-Koen had achieved in London 1948. Anyway, Devers continued with her success in Atlanta 1996, in which she obtained two other golds: she repeated on the hectometer and she joined the team that won the 4x100 relay. Happy with her brilliant career, the athlete wanted to give back some fortune, and in 1999 she created the Gail Devers Foundation, a charitable organisation to assist poor children with serious illnesses like the one she had to overcome.

POWER OF A WOMAN

Chinese female shooter Shan Zhang left all the gentlemen behind in the skeet contest on 28 July at the Mollet Olympic Tir Camp. Zhang, twenty-four, surpassed Peru's Juan Giha and Italian Bruno Rossetti (winner of silver and bronze, respectively) by 1 point and became the first 'golden' woman in this event, which until that edition was mixed.

'I have not come to Barcelona just to compete, I have come to win the gold medal,' said the oriental shooter, who in the last round crushed the other four finalists, all men, and came to be considered the best in the world. The Chinese revealed that the secret of her success was to play basketball, because that sport allowed her to train the coordination between eyes and limbs. In the following Games, Atlanta 1996, this specialty was divided into two categories, one male and one female. The IOC said that this decision had been taken before Barcelona and it was not related to any misogynistic speculation aimed at avoiding new embarrassing situation for men.

BOXER WITHOUT GLOVES

Iranian boxer Ali Kazemi started very poorly on the morning of 29 July. He woke up late, delayed with his breakfast, and when he went to board the bus that was to transport him from the Olympic Village to the Pavelló Club Joventut Badalona, the boy discovered alarmed that it had already left. Desperate, Kazemi miraculously got a taxi that took him at full speed to the stadium where he had to face Pakistani national, Mohammad Asghar, in the first round of the tournament for the light-heavyweight category. Upon arrival, the Iranian paid the fee, hurried down from the car and showed up for the fight in just the right time. However, upon entering the changing room, Kazemi was shocked to see that he had forgotten his gloves in the taxi, nervous about reaching on time. Without those basics for combat, the unfortunate Iranian was disqualified. The day, which had started badly, ended worse.

DOPED PODIUM

For a competition that proposes respect for the rules and regulations, and manifests itself against drugs, it could be considered bizarre that the three medalists of the same contest have been athletes with a history of doping. The unusual case occurred on 31 July at the Estadi Olímpic de Montjuïc, where the men's shot-put tournament was held. The winner was the American Michael Stulce, who had just served a two-year sentence of suspension for the use of testosterone. The silver medal was held by James Doehring, twin of the champion: also Yankee, also sentenced two years for using testosterone. The Russian national Vyacheslav Lykho, third and winner of bronze, got a relatively leniant punishment: he had suffered a three-month severance for consumption of another prohibited substance.

Doehring, on the other hand, carried an additional weight on his shoulders: seven months before the Games, he declared himself 'guilty' in a trial for amphetamine possession. A federal magistrate sentenced him to 6 months in jail in a semi-open prison, 5 years of probation and 125 hours of community work. But before sealing his sentence with a hammer blow, the judge authorised his trip to the Mediterranean metropolis and claimed the insurgent athlete to train 'hard for the Olympics.' Doehring, grateful, obeyed and returned home with the accomplished goal.

TANTRUM

The judges were surprised by the unusual gesture of the Czech national Ibrahim Samadov during the light-heavyweight weightlifting event. The lifter of the 'unified team' refused to have his bronze medal hung on his neck and left the Pavelló de l'Espanya Industrial, venue of the contest, on 3 August. No one knew the reason that justified that attitude, since no irregularity had happened during the tournament. The IOC representatives, severe, disqualified Samadov and suspended him for life to compete in the Games. 'Samadov was upset with his own performance, not with the judges, and on the podium he refused to put the medal on him and agreed to only receive it in his hand. Then he left the medal on the ground and left,' the IOC spokeswoman Sandrine Tonge said to the press. Apparently, the Czechen was upset because the competition had been defined by body weight. All three winners—he, the Greek-Albanian Pyrros Dimas and the Polish Krzysztof Siemion—had added 370 kilos with their lifts. As required by the regulations, in case of a tie, the winner is the lightest participant. Samadov, the heaviest of the three, was on the last step of the podium. Upon knowing about the life ban, the Czechen regretted his reaction, apologised and requested that his medal be reinstated, but the IOC remained strict. The disrespectful attitude had been seen by 4000 spectators present in the stadium and millions more on television.

THE LIBERATING LADY

Runner Hassiba Boulmerka obtained the first Olympic gold medal for her country, Algeria, winning the 1500-meter race on 8 August. The proud champion, however, would have preferred to dedicate her trophy to another nation, France, where she had taken refuge. In her birthland, Boulmerka had to tolerate harsh criticism and even attacks from intolerant Islamic fundamentalists. When she ran through the streets of her hometown, Constantine, the young woman received constant insults, spit, and even was accused of a supposed 'heresy' of running in shorts in sight of men, and refusing to wear the veil in public events. After suffering a death threat from a radical group, Boulmerka moved to France, where she consolidated as a middle-distance runner. In addition to the gold medal in Barcelona, she was champion in the 1500 meters in the Tokyo and Gothenburg World Cups. Crowned with olives and owner of a prestigious reputation, Hassiba returned to Algeria to promote sports among girls and adolescents and combat the rigid social regulations prevailing in that state of North Africa.

JOHNSON, OUT AGAIN

The rehabilitated Canadian sprinter Ben Johnson appeared twice in headlines during the Barcelona Games. First, for his bad performance: he qualified neither for the finals of the 100 meters nor the 4x100 relay. Second, because he again starred in a scandal that earned him the expulsion from the Olympic Village, although for reasons very different from those of Seoul 1988. Although the Jamaican-born runner, who in Spain showed his face with a permanent gesture of bad humour, was staying in a luxurious hotel, he was able to use the services of the Olympic Village like any other participant. On 9 August, the last day of the Games, Johnson wanted to share the day with some of his teammates, but forgot his acreditation. Upset because he was not allowed to enter directly, the sprinter agreed that the managers of the villa would issue a daily pass before giving him access. Shortly after, a volunteer claimed the authorisation at the door of one of the dining rooms. The sprinter, already furious for not being recognised, exploded in an attack of anger, took the boy by the neck and knocked him down. The incident mobilised a group of police officers who, after taking a statement from Johnson and his victim, ordered the athlete to leave the place. A farewell that did not contrast with the Jamaican Olympic performance.

ATLANTA 1996

Unlike the previous edition, the Centennial Games held in the American city Atlanta have a very bad reputation—firstly because the capital of the state of Georgia prevailed over Athens in the election of the host city. For many sports analysts, the power of the huge multinational companies that had their headquaters there (like Coca-Cola, also a sponsor of the Games) prevailed in the decision of the IOC over the vast history and sports legacy of Greece. And secondly, because the hundreds of organisational problems faced during the two weeks of the competition. Transportation, security, accommodation in the Olympic Village and the schedules of the various sports were not up to the mark, especially for a country listed as the richest and most powerful in the world.

The operational protection of athletes and the public was also very poor. On the day of the opening ceremony, on 19 July, a man dressed as a guard slipped into the Olympic stadium, named Turner Field, and wandered around the official box armed with a 45-caliber pistol. The intruder was discovered and arrested minutes before the arrival of national, local and IOC authorities, including US President Bill Clinton. A week later, an unbalanced guy identified as Eric Robert Rudolph blew up a homemade bomb in the Centennial Olympic Park, a site near the colosseum. The explosive unleashed a flurry of nails, screws and other projectiles that killed a woman and wounded another hundred. In addition, a Turkish television cameraman died of a heart attack while working there. Expert reports determined that the perpetrator was a former military officer expelled from the army for drug use.

On a strictly sporting department, the United States once again finished at the top position of the medal table after its 'failures' in Seoul and Barcelona. The local team added 101 medals (44 golds, 32 silvers and 25 bronzes), followed by Germany, with 65, and Russia, with 63. However, the Russian team obtained more gold medals (26) than the German (20).

On 3 August, at the Stanford Stadium of the city of Athens (from Georgia, not from Greece), Nigeria defeated Argentina 3–2 and became the first African football team to win an intercontinental tournament of this sport in the top men's category. Until then, all the World Cups and Olympic championships had been left to European and South American countries.

EXPELLED FOR A SMELL

According to an information from the ANSA agency, Turkey's national skeet champion, Aleadin Yatalakoglu, was expelled from the Olympic team by the authorities of the Shooting Federation for an unclean custom: throwing 'noisy farts' during training. The unusual decision was adopted at the request of Yatalakoglu's own companions, who refused to smell the aromatic effects of the shooter during their stay in Atlanta. Speaking to the *Hurriyet* newspaper, the accused admitted that he did not bother to retain his gases in front of his comrades, but he considered that 'farting is not a sufficient reason' to be banished from the Games. Turkey did not present any competitor for skeet contest at the Wolf Creek complex, but Yatalakoglu's absence allowed, as a counterpart, the rest of the delegation a pleasant and fragrant stay at the Olympic Village.

BIG PROBLEM

Champion in the amateur world tournament of Berlin 1995 and in the Mar del Plata Pan American Games of the same year, the American boxer Antonio Deon Tarver, was the great favourite to keep the gold in the light-heavyweight category—until McDonald's hamburgers were crossed on his way. The African-American boxer, a lover of cheeseburgers and the Big Mac, was dazzled by the restaurant located inside the Olympic Village, completely free for athletes. From his first day in the complex, Tarver took full advantage of the free meals and devoured dozens of sandwiches until his coach, alarmed, ended the gastronomic party. In just a few days, the boxer had increased three and a half kilos and had exceeded the weight limit of his category. Subjected to a rigid fast, Tarver qualified with the right weight but the diet, unlike the McDonald's stand, did pass the bill: the violent continence had greatly deteriorated his physical condition. In the first fight, the American defeated the Russian international Dmitry Vybornov by a narrow margin. Then, helped by an intake of salads and pasta, he surpassed David Kowah, from Sierra Leone, and Enrique Flores, from Puerto Rico. 'It wasn't my fault, it was McDonald's,' Tarver apologised for not having reached a higher place on the podium.

DISTRACTED

Georgian judoka Davit Khakhaleishvili trained for four years to defend his golden title of Barcelona 1992 in the top men's category. However, on the morning of 20 July, a strange blend of confusion and mistakes resulted in his disqualification in the Games. First, the fighter missed the special transport that was to run from the Olympic

Village to the Georgia World Congress Center for the official weighing. Very nervous and with a poor management of the English language, the Georgian obtained information from a volunteer and ran to take the metropolitan train, but the boy had told him the direction to another Olympic field! From there, the judoca received the appropriate directives and boarded a train of the correct line, although confused with the names of the stations, he descended at a wrong stop. Khakhaleishvili returned to the platform, boarded another train and finally arrived at the Georgia World Congress Center for weighing but he could not enter, because he had forgotten his official identification in his room. On the edge of despair, he got into a taxi to go to the Villa and return to the stadium, but the chaotic traffic of Atlanta killed his dream altogether. When the champion of Barcelona finally managed to enter the stadium, he had already been disqualified for absence and the judges had given the match to his rival, the Romanian Alexandru Lungu. 'I don't know if I want to continue living. I feel that four years of training and sweating are worthless than anything,' the disconsolate judoka of Eastern Europe sobbed.

THEY BEAT HIM OUT OF FATIGUE

In the Olympic Games there have been dozens of very even races on the track or the pool, although few like the one played by the swimmers Jani Sievinen (Finn) and Paul Palmer (British) in one of the preliminary races of the 200-meter freestyle for men. On the morning of 20 July, at the pool of the Georgia Tech Aquatic Center, Sievinen and Palmer intervened in the fourth qualifying series, and the two crossed the four stretchs in 1:49.5. The remarkable equality placed the two competitors in eighth place, so both had to take part in a tiebreaker to join the other seven swimmers who would compete in the final in the afternoon. Shortly before noon, the Finn and the British threw themselves into the water together, and believe it or not, they tied again but with a different time: 1:48.89. After a long reflection, the judges determined that the boys would again compete with each other until one gets advantage over the other. However, the third duel was not necessary, because Sievinen, exhausted and aware that he would have little time to recover for the final, preferred to resign. With the road smoothed, Palmer participated in the final race, but so tired that he finished in the last position.

NAKED CELEBRATION

To celebrate the triumph in the Olympic women's football championship, the goalkeeper of the US national team, the brunette Briana Scurry, twenty-four years old, took an Olympic lap, 'dressed' only with her gold medal. A couple of hours after the 2–1 victory over China was sealed at Sanford Stadium in the city of Athens, Georgia, Scurry got into a friend's car, looked for a clear area of walkers, undressed and jogged with her prize around her neck, protected by the darkness of the night. Meanwhile, her partner recorded the celebration with a video camera, with special shots of a panther tattoo attached to the left shoulder of the goalkeeper. 'I had made this promise and I wanted to keep it. We have recorded a tape as evidence, but nobody will see it,' Scurry slipped gracefully when interviewed on a television channel. Eight years later, casually in Athens (the Greek city), the 'panther' repeated her gold against Brazil, but not her crazy celebration.

FROM BEGGAR TO MILLIONAIRE

In 1995, Alvin Harrison and his twin brother Calvin lived inside an old black Ford Mustang car parked in front of Monterey Bay in California. After a childhood in a poor district of Orlando, where they were raised by their grandmother, the boys, who in high school had stood out as sprinters, had hit rock bottom. Both worked with hazardous waste and had their meals at cheap fast food restaurants, until Alvin, who did not know the meaning of the word 'surrender', decided to sign up for a pre-Olympic competition in the city of Reno, Nevada. Despite not being properly prepared, the young man won the 400-meter contest with an extraordinary record, which caught the attention of a representative of the Nike sportswear company. The executive hired him and incorporated him to an Oregon athletic team. Alvin continued with incredible progress, and a few months after living on the street, he joined the US Olympic team. In Atlanta, Harrison came fourth in the 400-meter final, but he contributed exceptionally to the local team winning the gold in the 4x400 relay. For the 2000 Sydney Games, Calvin joined the team, and with the Harrison brothers, the United States repeated gold in the relay race. Alvin, who covered the first quarter, and Calvin, the third, became the first pair of twins to win the gold medal together in an Olympic athletic event. To their misfortune, one of their companions, Antonio Pettigrew, admitted eight years later to have used prohibited drugs for that race. The IOC disqualified the American quartet and withdrew the gold. It was a black outcome, although not as much as that car where the brothers had to live before twisting their own destiny.

SYDNEY 2000

The Games returned to the southern hemisphere for the second time after forty-four years, and Australia was once again the country chosen to host the great sporting event. In Athens, the Greeks, who had wanted to organise the Centennial Olympiad, came back to bite the dust. The Hellenes wished to be compensated for the 1996 snub with the 'Jubilee Game', but they lost again, this time, said the rumors, against the economic power of an Australian pharmaceutical consortium. Several media investigation questioned the election of the biggest nation of Oceania and claimed to have seen the president of the IOC, Juan Antonio Samaranch, handling the threads as a puppeteer master. Beyond this controversy, in the strictly sporting plane, Sydney was a host of excellence, where all the ceremonies and tournaments were perfectly coordinated to give rise to a splendid party.

The medal table was dominated again by the United States team, which was left with 94 medals (37 golds, 24 silvers and 33 bronzes). Russia totaled 89 and China, a giant that was beginning to wake up, 58.

At the Penrith Lake racing center, English rower Stephen Redgrave won his fifth gold medal in five consecutive Games. Redgrave ranked first on the podium since Los Angeles 1984, although he won it in three different contests: pair-oared without coxswain and four-oared with/without coxswain. For his successes as an athlete, he received in 1987 the honourary title of Member of the British Empire and in 1997, that of Commander of the British Empire. In 2001, after his success achieved in Australia, he was appointed Knight.

A situation aroused a huge controversy: the Australian organisers disdained the rules of the IOC and allowed the official opening of the Games in charge of Governor General William Deane, and not as indicated by the protocol, in the presence of Queen Elizabeth of England, the corresponding Head of State. Isabel, indeed, had participated in the ceremony in Montreal. The only previous Olympic inaugurations that did not count on the presence of the monarch, president or first authority of the host country were San Luis 1904 (intervened by the administrator of the Universal Exhibition, David Rowland Francis), Los Angeles 1932 (headed by Vice President Charles Curtis) and, what a paradox, Melbourne 1956, where Isabel did not attend but her husband, Prince Philip of Edinburgh. Governor Deane also refused to deliver his speech in French, the official language of the Olympic movement. Samaranch implored Deane to have the courtesy of using both languages, but the governor abruptly rejected him. 'In Australia, we speak English,' he said.

THE FOOL OF THE CENTURY

The Andalusian thief walked around the arrival hall of the Seville airport snooping around for some abandoned foreign suitcase, or at least neglected some valuable moments, from which to seize and escape quickly to enjoy its valuable content. That morning, 17 August 1999, the boy, with his eyes in a state of maximum alert, came and went. He was convinced that some of the thousands of travelers crossing the hall would give some advantage to his hand, trained in the art of seizing other people's things. Then, his quick feet would complete the misdeed. The strategy-adrenaline-prize blend left him a greater revenue than the heavy and boring jobs he could access, and also offered him unparalleled excitement. After a long wander, eureka! Behind a column, a brightly coloured bag poked out of its owner's field of vision. The man, moreover, was absorbed in a talk with other people. Looking more closely, the rogue warned that his victim was actually interviewed by television journalists. 'Will that black man be someone important?', he asked quietly. Anyway, greed could be more than curiosity and the thief stained his loot and escaped straight, quickly heading for the exit, covered in the media confusion and confident in the lightness of his legs. If the little pirate had had as much knowledge of sport as of crime, he would have noticed that his tall and muscular black target was Maurice Greene, nothing less than the fastest athlete in the world. The rascal put his best energy and enthusiasm in his running scape, but everithing was in vain: he was an easy prey for the famous sprinter. In a couple of seconds, Greene pulverized the disadvantage meters, reached the criminal and immobilized him with his powerful arms. He immediately handed it over to two Civil Guard uniformed officers who took the robber under arrest to the local police station. A few days later, inside his damp cell, the unfortunate crook could not believe the information that came from the radio: the man he had wanted to steal had been world champion after winning the 100 and 200-meter races in the Olympic Stadium of the Cartuja. The American sprinter would repeat the gold on the hectometer a year later, at the Sydney Olympics. Crumpled in the dungeon, the thief had no doubts. If he had to plead guilty about something, it was to be incredibly stupid.

THE IMPOSTOR

When on 19 September the Australian swimmer returned to the Olympic Village, he found a surprise: the guards did not allow him to pass because, according to their records, he was already inside the small athletic town. The boy, very amused, explained to the guards that it must have been a mistake because till then he had been competing inside the Sydney International Aquatic Center. The uniformed found that what the swimmer said was true, and after conducting a quick investigation, determined that an intruder had mocked the controls with a false credential that had the same barcode as that of the athlete. The strangest case was that the competitor in question was Ian Thorpe, the highest Olympic champion in the history of his country with 9 medals (5 golds, 3 silvers and 1 bronze). Thorpe did not understand how the guards—countrymen of him—had not identified the intruder or recognised his face that, by those days, appeared hundreds of times in street posters, newspaper advertisements and television ads.

MARITAL DUEL

In Sydney 2000 there was an unprecedented event in the history of Olympic sport: the members of a marriage faced each other. This situation is even more unusual if you take into account that it was starred by handball players Camilla Andersen, a twenty-seven-year-old Danish woman, and Mia Hundvin, a Norwegian girl of twenty-three. These ladies, who had started their love relationship when they were both in the ranks of the Danish club Frederiksberg Idræts Forening (FIF), legalised their union a few months before traveling to Australia. On 17 September, the beautiful Camilla and Mia met on the court when their respective teams crossed into the opening game of group B. The first to smile was Mia—Norway won by 19–17 in a minor clash. The Scandinavians were the top two selected in a five-team zone, of which four qualified for the final draw. Six games later, on 1 October, the one who uncorked champagne was Camilla, after her squad surpassed Hungary, 31–27, in the final for the gold medal. Mia, meanwhile, did not return home with her hands empty: after having fallen to the Magyian team in the semi-finals, Norway beat South Korea 22–21 in the match for the third place and won the bronze. Despite the extraordinaryOlympic experience and having their home decorated with two valuable medals, the marriage broke three years later. The separation of the successful and beautiful sportsmen fed for weeks the covers of the tabloid press and the Nordic gossip magazines. However, the news of the divorce seemed just a little comment with the next step in the young Norwegian's sentimental life: Mia captured all the flashes when she began appearing in glamorous restaurants and trendy nightclubs with Terje Håkonsen, a tough footballer and famous snowboarding champion, a winter-extreme sport very popular in Scandinavia. In addition, to add fuel to the fire, the attractive player agreed to pose with little clothes for some publications. The media ended up exploding when Mia completed her 180-degree turn by becoming pregnant with the first of her two children. The girl, a true box of surprises, crowned her polemical 'reality' with a controversial statement to the women's magazine *KK*: 'I was married to a woman, but I have never considered myself to be gay either. When you have feeling for someone, you forget what gender the person is... Generally speaking, I don't think I will be with a woman again, but I have learned one thing; you never get any guarantees'. A phrase of bronze, like her medal.

EELS

In an alleged attempt to promote swimming in emerging countries, the IOC invited two boys from Equatorial Guinea, with almost no aquatic experience, to act in two competitions. Eric Moussambani, 22, intervened in the playoffs of the 100-meter freestyle. On 19 September, Moussambani threw himself into the pool of the Aquatic Center, and with a doggy- style splash, covered the course in 1:52.3. Several participants and even some spectators were about to jump into the water to rescue the African, who seemed about to drown. The winner of that test, the Dutchman Pieter van den Hoogenband, traveled that same distance in 48.30 seconds; the penultimate, the Qatari Dawood Youssef Mohamed Jassim, in 1:02.45. Three days later, Paula Barila Bolopa, eighteen, acted in the eliminator of the 50-meter freestyle with another ridiculous record: 1:3.97. The champion, also Dutch, Inge de Bruijn, took just 24.32 seconds; the penultimate, Aissatou Barry, of the Republic of Guinea, 35.79 seconds. 'She is worse than me,' shameless Moussambani mocked, whom his 'colleagues' had baptised him as 'the eel'.

INDOMITABLE LIONS

Cameroon's national football team was known with a fierce nickname: Indomitable Lions. The vibrant duel of the quarter-finals against Brazil justified this name. On 23 September, at Brisbane Cricket Ground, the African squad took advantage at 17 minutes through Patrick Mboma. Brazil could only punch the Cameroonian defense at the 94th minute—the added time seemed exaggerated—with a free kick by its great star Ronaldinho, and after the controversial German referee Herbert Fandel sent off two African players, Geremi Njitap and Aaron Nguimbat. After the questionable equality, the Brazilian team was in an unbeatable situation to seize in the extra time, with eleven players against only nine of Cameroon. However, the numerical disadvantage did not depress the 'lions'. Modeste M'bami scored an incredible winner in the 113th minute with a terrific shot from outside the penalty area. As at that time the 'golden goal'—which granted the victory to the team that made the first goal—was valid in the regulation, the brave team from Cameroon went to the semi-final on a historic and unforgettable day. Minutes after the defeat, the Brazilian coach Wanderley Luxembourg admitted to the press feeling 'shame' and asked for 'apologies from the

180 million Brazilians'. A few days later, Luxembourg was fired by the Brazilian Football Confederation and replaced by Felipe Scolari, who would lead the squad to their fifth world title in the tournament jointly organized by South Korea and Japan, in 2002.

INDOMITABLE FINAL

The final of the football tournament, played on 30 September between Spain and Cameroon at the Olympic stadium, was the most exciting in the history of the Games. The first half was fulfilled with a comfortable advantage for the European team by 2–0, which could have been extended if the African goalkeeper Idriss Kameni did not stop a penalty shot of Miguel Ángel Angulo. In the second half, the 'Indomitable Lions' achieved a heroic equality, supported by an unfortunate own goal by the Iberian Ivan Amaya. Spain also suffered the sent off of two players, Gabriel García de la Torre and José María Romero, but it was still inches away from winning the game with a 'golden goal' in the extra time, when a shot by Joan Capdevilla burst the Cameroonian crossbar. In the penalty shoot-out, Amaya, the antihero of the day, hit the crossbar. This was the only wrong shot, which allowed Cameroon to win the golden medal and match the feat that Nigeria had achieved four years earlier in Atlanta.

The team from Spain wore white—a colour they considered to transmit bad luck. Despite having won in the coin toss for the jersey, they had to waer their alternative jersey since Cameroon only had a set of dark green shirts. The Africans were sanctioned with a fine for not having alternative clothing, but that little mattered. They were already at the top of the podium. The depression came a few days later, upon learning that, for the silver medal, the Iberians received a reward of about 40,000 USD per head. Each of the champions got, barely, about 15,000 USD.

GOB

The American national, Amy Van Dyken, was very annoying. Although he had added two gold medals in the pool of the Sydney International Aquatic Center, those were in two group events: the 4x100 freestyle relay and 4x100 medley relay. Van Dyken wanted to repeat the gold in the 50-meter freestyle she had won in Atlanta, and her biggest enemy, Inge de Bruijn, was a very hard threat. The Dutch had already monopolised two individual successes in the 100-meter freestyle and the 100-meter butterfly, and in the preliminaries had been unbeatable. To disturb her rival, the American took advantage of the fact that both were in neighbouring platforms, and from her place, spat on the lane of the European. The vile maneuver was not only warned by De Bruijn, but by numerous spectators, who disapproved of the American's attitude with whistles and insults. In spite of the gob that floated in her dive sector, the Dutch was launched with great determination and won the race. Van Dyken, turned off by public censorship, barely finished fourth, with no place on the podium, no medal and burning jealousy. The American escaped from the complex without witnessing the awards ceremony. But, before disappearing, she fired thick ammunition against the Dutch woman when she met a journalist from her country: 'I could have won that if I were a man,' she bitchily commented.

ATHENS 2004

Finally it was Athens's turn! The Hellenic nation, cradle of the Olympic Games, had claimed with absolute justice to host in 1996, the year of the centenary. Then, in 2000, the end of the millennium. In both cases, powerful commercial consortiums imposed the obesity of their checkbooks so that the sacred Olympic flame traveled to Atlanta and to Sydney. The year 2004 did not imply any special date, which in some way can be seen as positive, because it will be remembered only as that of the Greek Olympiad. A highly praised fact was that the champion athletes, in addition to the famous medals, received olive crowns made with twigs from the sacred trees of Olympia.

In the final table, the United States, with 102 medals (36 golds), surpassed Russia, with 92 (27 golds). Although it did not reach one of the first places, Argentina was a pleasant surprise: it again received a gold medal after fifty-two years, twice, thanks to two male teams: in football, a sport in which the South American country had been world champion but not Olympic champion, and in basketball, after notably surpassing the American 'Dream Team' in the semi-finals and Italy in the great end.

Football, this time, brought some surprises. Iraq, a nation with no history of relevance, and just been invaded by the United States and other allied countries (supposedly for maintaining ties with the al-Qaeda terrorist organisation and a never-proven accusation of producing weapons of mass destruction), reached the semi-final and then fell just 1–0 to Italy in the duel for the bronze medal. Argentina, which finished the tournament without goals into its net, something that had never happened before, crushed Serbia and Montenegro on 11 August by 6–0. Two years later, in the 2006 World Cup in Germany, both teams met again and the clash culminated in the same unusual marker.

THE HIT

Kenyan light-flyweight boxer Suleiman Bilali Wanjau, who had reached the quarter-finals in Sydney 2000, was very well prepared to reach the podium in Athens. But, a few days after leaving for the Greek capital, his participation was knocked out because of a hit. Wanjau, who worked in Nairobi as a police officer, was shot during a bank robbery. The serious injury did not allow the fighter to recover in time to compete in the Athens Games. Wanjau was able to travel to Beijing, although his performance was very weak when he fell in his first fight with the Dominican, Winston Méndez Montero.

GLUTTONY STRIKE

Iranian judoka Arash Miresmaeili, world champion in the 66-kilos category and flag bearer of his country at the opening ceremony, was disqualified even before competing since he exceeded the official weight. Despite being eliminated without fighting, the twenty-three-year-old was happy and smiling. At first, no one understood the reason behind their satisfaction, but then it was learned that during the hours prior to climbing the scale, Miresmaeili had crammed himself with food in order to exceed the maximum limit of his category and be excluded. In this way, the Iranian avoided fighting in the first round with the Israeli Ehud Vaks, the rival that had corresponded to him by draw. An official of the Iranian sports delegation emphasised that 'our policy is not to recognise the Zionist regime in any international event. We cannot accept the presence of someone bearing that flag'. Meanwhile, the President of the Persian nation, Mohammad Khatami, said that Miresmaeili was considered 'the champion of the 2004 Olympic Games' and that his actions would be 'engraved in the history of the glories of Iran'. In a brief contact with international journalists, the judoca expressed his solidarity 'with the suffering of the people of Palestine' and admitted not feeling 'upset at all' with his disqualification. It was no wonder that he was happy: President Khatami had ordered that a reward equivalent to 125,000 USD be given to judoca, the amount agreed upon for athletes who obtained gold medals in Athens.

I DECLARE YOU 'HUSBAND AND WIFE AND RIVALS'!

A very particular situation took place in the equestrian center of Markopoulos: a man and his wife met for the first time in an Olympic event. Although there was a precedent of crossings between the two members of a marriage, it had had to do with two women married to each other: handball players Camilla Andersen, from Denmark, and Mia Hundvin, from Norway. Until 15 August, it had never happened that husband and wife competed against each other in the dispute of a medal. The curious situation corresponded to the Australian Andrew Hoy, forty-one, and Germany's Bettina Overesch-Böker, forty-one, who participated in the three-day equestrian contest: dressage, eventing and jumping. While Andrew and Bettina had confronted at other Games, in Athens they did so for the first time as spouses. Although the husband added three golds and one silver in three previous Games, against a single bronze of his partner, this time it was she who went further in the general table. Bettina finished eighth, while Andrew left before completing his routine. At the end of the contest, the Hoys returned to their home that, as good competitors, they had made on neutral ground: Great Britain.

IGNORANT REFEREE

In Athens, FIFA continued its unbearable habit of appointing referees from countries with little or no football tradition for important matches. In the group clash between Serbia and Montenegro and Tunisia, which defined the classification to the second round (the African squad had to win by a bulky score and expect Argentina to beat Australia by several goals), the judge chosen was Charles Ariiotima. The official game form indicated that the referee was of Tahitian nationality, which was incorrect because Tahiti is only the largest of the islands of French Polynesia, which is not an independent state but a French overseas territory located in the Pacific Ocean. Either way, Tahitian, Polynesian or French, Ariiotima—a man who worked as a plumber—showed that he was not adequately prepared to handle the spirit of football regulation, much less to lead in a high-level championship. On 17 August, at the Pampeloponnisiako stadium in the city of Patras, located 200 kilometers from Athens, Balkans and Africans were 1–1 until 78th minute, when the referee whistled a penalty for Tunisia. The execution was taken by Mohamed Jedidi, who shot and defeated goalkeeper Nikola Milojevic. But, while the Africans celebrated, Ariiotima annulled the goal by the alleged invasion of a Tunisian player on the Serbian area. Jedidi took the shot again, the ball came back in and the Tahitian referee again invalidated the goal by an alleged infringement of an African. The story did not end there. The penalty was executed and repeated three more times, among which twice, though was stopped by Milojevic, the referee believed that the keeper had advanced before the shooting. The incredible situation made the 7000 spectators laugh and drove players, coaches and substitutes from both teams crazy. No one understood anything. To make matters worse, Ariiotima was supported by two linesmen that, due to their inexperience and limited liveliness to apply the regulation, generated more problems than solutions: Tony Meltetamat and Michael Mouauri, representatives of two Pacific archipelagos, Vanuatu and Cook Islands, whose football leagues were lowercase. After ten minutes of parody, Jedidi kicked his sixth penalty—strong and in the middle, far from the reach of Milojevic, who had flown to his left—and the Polynesian referee validated the goal convinced that the procedure has been done according to the rules. The teammates of the scorer, just in case, had been waiting in the middle of the pitch.

The Tunisian team finally won by 3–2, but was eliminated because Australia only fell 1–0 against Argentina. Ariiotima did not arbitrate again in Greece and returned home to continue his work as a plumber.

UNUSUAL FORGETS

The walker Francisco Javier Fernández Peláez, simply 'Paquillo' for the Spaniards, reaffirmed hundreds of times before arriving in Greece that his objective was to compete and not to win a medal. 'I can be fifth,' he warned. However, his performance in Athens was worthy of the podium, finishing second in the 20,000-metre walk. After his success, Paquillo offered a press conference in which, in fact, he showed that the medal had never been an obsession. When the interrogation of journalists ended, the athlete stood up from his chair and left…without his trophy! When one of the reporters mentioned it, the Spaniard concluded with laughter that 'sometimes I forget it'.

Much more serious was the case of Chilean tennis player Nicolás Massú, who won only two gold medals in the Olympic history of Chile in a period of just eight hours. Massú—champion in individual and in doubles, along with Fernando González—left Athens and left his two golds in a drawer of his room in the Olympic Village. The prizes were rescued by the coach of the swimming team of the South American country and handed to González, who returned them to Massú when they both met in the US Open in New York.

Another dumb, Dutch rower Diederik Simon, left his silver medal in the taxi seat that he took from the Olympic Village to the Farilo nightclub area. A while later, the driver of the vehicle discovered the medal and returned it to an employee of the local Olympic committee, who rewarded the taxi driver's decency with a cash prize.

THE MAN WITH TWO PENISES

The throw of the Hungarian Róbert Fazekas was fantastic. The discus flew over 70.93 meters and set a new Olympic record. Fazekas, with a huge smile, received his gold medal and enjoyed how the melody of the magyar anthem filled the great Spyridon Louis Stadium in honour of the famous marathon runner. A few minutes after the awards ceremony, the 1.93-meter tall and 114-kilogram big man was summoned to the office for the anti-doping controls. The discobolus entered without objections in a cabinet to deposit a sample of urine inside the official jar that had been delivered to him. However, the doctor in charge of the procedure noticed something abnormal in the giant body. As he approached to the athlete, he observed that Fazekas was holding his penis—which peeked through one of the sleeves of the shorts—with one hand to pee into the glass container held with the other extremity, but in his inner thigh was a suspicious lump. The doctor demanded that the Hungarian undress completely, which revealed an original trap: the athlete had two phallus, the natural one and a rubber one loaded with 'clean' urine so that the prohibited substances that he had consumed to win the tournament could not affect the drug test. Fazekas was denounced and disqualified. The IOC forced him to return the gold medal and erased the mark from its records. The triumph corresponded, then, to the Lithuanian Virgilijus Alekna, who thus repeated his 2000 Sydney title.

ABUSIVE COACH

To aspire for a medal, South Korean Ye Geu-Rim could not lose to Germany's Julia Matijass, in the lighter category of the female judo tournament. Ye had fallen to the Chinese Gao Feng in a preliminary fight and a second defeat left her out of the contest. Before getting on the tatami, the girl was approached by the coach of the Korean team, Suh Jung-Bok, who told her a series of precise and complicated directives. But Ye, bent by the superiority of the German, could not deploy anything that Suh had advised. After leaving the tatami, the defeated Ye was insulted by her coach, who also launched a slap that hit the face of the girl in view of the public, the judges and the rest of the participants. The rude Suh was immediately expelled from the Ano Liossia Stadium and forced to leave the Olympic Village and Greece on the same day. 'We do not tolerate these attitudes,' said the director of the International Judo Federation, Michel Brousse. Although she was doubly hurt by the elimination and the beating blow, poor Ye enjoyed at least one consolation prize—she could do away with her coach's company.

ACID LIME

The Brazilian long-distance runner Vanderlei Lima led the marathon that was played on 29 August with almost a minute of advantage over the Italian Stefano Baldini. At the height of kilometer 36, a half-crazy Irish intruder called Cornelius Horan, known throughout Europe for breaking into various sports competitions with quirky clothes, got in the way of the South American athlete. Horan appeared from the left of Lima, hugged him and pushed him toward the fence that contained the spectators. The incident lasted just two seconds, but that was enough to cut the concentration of the Brazilian. Demoralised by the occurrence of the Irish, Lima was surpassed by Baldini and the American Mebrahtom Keflezighi, who won the gold and silver medals, respectively. Lima kept at least the bronze medal, but after the end, he protested the result and claimed to be recognised as the winner of the race. The athlete had only reported safety deficiencies in the course, an aspect that exceeded the reach of that institution. The International Olympic Committee, meanwhile, eluded the eventuality with elegance: it gave Lima the honourable medal 'Pierre de Coubertin', reserved for excelent sportmen and which only nine other athletes had accessed throughout history. Back at home, the unfortunate marathoner received 67,000 USD from the 'Pao de Açúcar' group, sponsor of the Brazilian Olympic team, the same amount that the other gold medalists charged. Other sponsors reacted the same way. But for Lima, all these affectionate tributes were not enough to dissolve the bitterness of not having imposed his name on the marble of the Olympic champions. An anguish exacerbated by the fact that Horan, responsible for destroying his dreams and the effort of a lifetime, was not even punished. The Irishman was released immediately, absolved after paying a ridiculous bond of 3000 euros.

BEIJING 2008

The great Beijing Games can be defined with two monosyllables, Phelps and Bolt, the last names of the two athletes who, in the capital of the People's Republic of China, achieved a unique performance in the Olympic history. The American swimmer Michael Phelps took part in eight races: he won eight with seven world records and surpassed the harvest of his countryman and colleague Mark Spitz, who had won seven golds in Munich 1972. Phelps prevailed in the 200-meter freestyle, the 100- and 200-meter butterfly, the 200- and 400-meter medley (all individual triumphs) and the 4x100 and 4x200 freestyle and 4x100 medley relays.

The Jamaican sprinter Usain Bolt, meanwhile, ran in three races, in all three he broke the world record and became the fastest man on the planet. The Caribbean won the triple speed crown in the 100 and 200 meter and the 4x100 relay. Interestingly, Bolt broke a year later his own records of 100 and 200 meters at the World Cup in Berlin.

Beyond these two unique performances, Beijing was the scene of 36 new world marks and 143 Olympics, a remarkable situation for such an advanced modern edition. In addition, eighty-six countries won medals, something that had never happened before. Yet there was tension regarding the climatic condition of the host metropolis. However, the alleged high air pollution did not seem to affect the participants or the spectators, which also, although not perspiring, reached a record: tickets for all specialties were sold out, something that had never happened in a Game. In total, seven million tickets were sold for the 302 competitions, and all the oriental stadiums were filled. For Athens 2004, the previous edition, only two thirds of the tickets had been sold. The contests also had a spectacular setting, with top-level scenarios among which the 'Water Cube', home of swimming contests, and the Bird's Nest, the new Olympic stadium so called for its colourful steel net inits exterior covered by a transparent membrane, which was the home of athletics and the final of the football tournament that Argentina won with Lionel Messi in its team.

The medalist table was led by the United States team, with 110 (36 golds, 38 silvers and 36 bronzes), followed by China, with 100. Of course, if a higher value is given to the gold medals, the local squad was the winner, with 51.

AGAINST SNOW AND RAIN

The Olympic fire is sacred. The flames that have been illuminating the Games since 1936—when the German historian Carl Diem came up with the idea of adapting the ancient legend of Prometheus, the titan who stole the fire from the gods and gave it to humans—must travel from Olympia to the main stadium of each host city without extinguishing and it should stay alive until the end of the competitions. For the Berlin edition, a magnesium-fed torch was used and over the years the beacons and their power source were modernised according to the routes by land, sea and air. The goal of such technological attention is simply to prevent the extinguishing flame: according to a legend, the Games would be cursed by the gods, and some misfortune could happen to the athletes if that happens. To avoid any 'tragic' outcome, the candle is accompanied by several closed lanterns that are used to turn it on again when some special contingency happens, such as when boarding an airplane. Open fire is not allowed inside the aircraft, for safety reasons.

For this oriental edition, the International Olympic Committee arranged for a team of 10 technicians to accompany the torch to watch over its flame during the tour of 135 cities in 20 countries, along 137,000 kilometers. But, to prevent any carelessness, the torch of these Games was specially designed by the China Aerospace Corporation with a propane tank that allowed it to stay lit in all kinds of weather conditions. Prepared to withstand high winds and heavy rains, the flame passed victoriously through London, where its route was decorated by heavy snowfall.

STRANGELY UNIQUE

The city of Beijing was prepared to be the first edition of the Games in which all the countries affiliated to the International Olympic Committee (IOC) partcipated. The president of the IOC, the Belgian Jacques Rogge, had predicted that 'nobody is going to miss' the sport party. However, this long-awaited desire could not be realized, because of the clumsiness of the leaders of the Sultanate of Brunei. In more than a hundred years of Olympic history, Brunei, a country with little sports tradition, presented a single athlete in Atlanta 1996 (Prince Abdul Hakeem, eliminated in the first round of the skeet shooting tournament), two in Sydney 2000 (the sprinter Haseri Asli, knocked out in the 100-meter qualification and again Prince Hakeem, again defeated in the preliminary round) and one in Athens 2004 (Jimmy Anak Ahar, who did not overtake the first classification test of the 1500-meter track race). For the Beijing edition, the small state of Southeast Asia had planned to register two athletes: fifteen-year-old swimmer Maria Grace Koh and shot-putter Mohammed Yazid Yatimi Yusof, twenty. But the Brunean Olympic leaders slacked off and the shortlist did not arrive in time to the offices of the IOC for their corresponding accreditation. 'It is a great shame and something very painful for athletes who are left out by this decision of their team not to register them. The IOC tried until the last moment to do so, but without result,' said the spokeswoman for the agency, Emmanuelle Moreau. Koh and Yusof, who had traveled to the Chinese capital, were left out of the parade along the 'Bird's Nest' track.

RUNNING FROM THE JAW OF LION

Ethiopian athlete Kenenisa Bekele landed in Beijing with an impeccable background to keep the gold medals in the 5000 and 10,000 meters. Indeed, Bekele was the holder of the world records in the two events, and he had also won a silver and a gold medal in Athens 2004, in the same disciplines. On the track of the Bird's Nest, the African did not disappoint his followers and seized gold in both races, with an Olympic record in the most extensive of them. How did a man who was born in the worst of misery and suffered hunger during his childhood attain Olympic glory and become one of the best runners of all time? In Ethiopia, jokes were made about the athlete's ability and the ferocity of the lions of that country. According to Bekele himself, once training with his brother Tariku in the mountainous area of Entoto, on the outskirts of Addis Ababa, the capital of the East African nation, the runner came to a lion cub. Immediately, the two boys noticed that, a few meters away, the jealous mother of the little animal was approaching with gestures that were far from friendly. Faced with the imminent danger, the brothers escaped at full speed, and just stopped their run after traveling a few kilometers. 'I was a little scared, since I had heard stories that a lioness is furious if she thinks something can harm her cub,' the athlete told a local newspaper after his alarming encounter. His national fans say that, after having escaped from the lions' claws, the fast runner has no one to fear on the track.

BAD LOSER

Surely, the Cuban taekwondist Ángel Matos knew the stories of several Olympic boxers who had protested the sentences of the referees with blowes when he decided to repeat this shameful way to complain. The Caribbean fighter—thirty-one years old and winner of the gold in Sydney 2000—did not accept to be disqualified by the Swedish judge Chekir Chelbat and expressed his whole anger with what he did best: to kick. The incident took place on 23 August in the gymnasium of the University of Science and Technology, where the Cuban faced the Kazakh Arman Chilmanov for the bronze medal in the highest category for men over 80 kilos. In the middle of the fight, Matos—who surpassed his rival in the scoreboard by 3–2—suffered a foot injury and was treated by doctors from his country. But when he returned to the arena to continue, Chelbat had finished the contest and declared the Kazakh as winner. The judge explained to the Cuban that his doctors had taken 62 seconds to practice healing, just two more than the time allowed by the rules. Matos, furious at the regulatory severity of the Swede, replied with a kick to the referee's head. Then, punched another judge in the arm and spat on the floor of the arena. The Caribbean coach, Leudis González, was not far behind: after protesting, insulting and also trying to resolve the issue with blows, he denounced to the press that the Kazakhstan team had tried to 'buy' the fight. 'The Kazakhs bribed the judges. They had offered me money first and I refused, so the referee was logically bought', Gonzalez shot. His accusation fell on deaf ears, and he and Matos were disqualified from the contest and suspended for life by the International Taekwondo Federation. An exemplary penalty for an infamous reaction.

THINGS MONEY CAN'T BUY

The Bahraini Olympic Committee—from a tiny but very rich kingdom of the Persian Gulf—decided to change its history at any cost. After six Games without obtaining any medal, it was resolved that if there were no elite athletes among the million inhabitants to obtain good results in Beijing, they would import from the neighbouring nations. The power of the petroUSD allowed that—of the 14 athletes sent to China, only three were born in Bahrain: the sprinter Rakia Al-Gassra, the swimmer Omar Jasim and the shooter Salman Zaman. Al-Gassra, who was the flag-bearer of the delegation, became famous for competing with long-sleeved trousers and shirts and a veil covering her head, according to the Muslim dress code known as 'hijab'. Of course, the cloak, decorated with the famous logo of Nike, did not seem very religious.

Of the rest of the participants, six were born in Kenya, three in Morocco, one in Jordan and one in Ethiopia. All foreigners were registered with Arabic names, in some cases other than the denominations with which the boys had been baptised. With almost 80 per cent of its foreign troops, Bahrain sent to China the largest and most expensive representation in its history…to achieve the usual result: zero medals. As the advertising of a credit card asserts, 'There are some things money can't buy'.

REVENGE WAS TERRIBLE

On 28 March 2007, during the world championship held in Melbourne, Australia, French swimmer Laure Manaudou snatched the world record in the 200-meter freestyle from her Italian colleague Federica Pellegrini. Manaudou celebrated her conquest with mocking glances at Pellegrini, who had stayed on the third step of the podium. Although inside boiled with anger, the Italian was stoic despite the bad time. She had plenty of time to diagram an atrocious 'vendetta'. Pellegrini's first step was to seduce her enemy's boyfriend, the Italian and also a swimmer, Luca Marin. The soap opera occupied dozens of pages in the yellow media of Europe, with photos of the 'happy couple' and the acrid gesture of the spiteful. The second phase was to train very hard for the Beijing Games, as never before. The arduous preparation paid off on 13 August : at the end of the 200 meters, Pellegrini won the gold medal and regained her world record. The only thing that the Italian regretted was that her retaliation could not be completed, because she did not face Manaudou to enjoy her facial expression. Her antagonist, perhaps prudent, had not qualified for that test.

KNOCKOUT WITHOUT FIGHT

American bantamweight boxer Gary Russell Jr. got an unusual knockout...about himself. Russell, two-time amateur champion in his country, arrived in China with excess weight, so he imposed himself a very strong fasting of food and drinks to put his body below the 54 kilo-limit. But the violent diet was so disastrous for the fighter, that he was found fainted in his room floor by one of his companions on the day of the official weighing. The young athlete was treated by doctors from the North American delegation, but failed to recover in time to compete in the Olympiad. Russell's absence, who was believed to be a serious gold candidate, opened the door of triumph for the Mongolian Enkhbatyn Badar-Uugan.

DISOBEDIENT

Scottish tennis player Andrew Murray ignored his mother. The woman wanted her son, number 6 in the world ranking, not to attend Beijing and prepare properly for the United States Open, the fourth and last of the prestigious tournaments that make up the Grand Slam every year. However, Murray disregarded his mother's advice and traveled to China to represent Britain in singles and doubles. 'I think she is wrong. Obviously it makes it harder, but there are three weeks between the two finals and we will have at least two weeks off in that time because we only play every second day,' said the rebel player three days before the start of the tournament, for which he looked with one foot on the podium. But reality hit him with a racket in the head: in singles, he lost in the first round with a stranger, Lu Yen-Hsun, from Taipei. In doubles, along with his brother Jamie, the Scotsman was eliminated in the second round, against the French Arnaud Clément and Michaël Llodra.

To avoid his mother's reprimand, Murray went directly to New York to participate in the Open held at the Billie Jean King National Tennis Center, in the district of Queens. There, perhaps rested by his expeditious failure in China, Murray reached the final of the important tournament, in which he was defeated by the Roger Federer (gold medal in doubles in China) in three sets. So yes, the Scot traveled home to celebrate his good performance with his wise mother.

LONDON 2012

Amazing for its staging, surprising for its call, extraordinary for its egalitarian character, London 2012, the third edition organised by the British capital, was shown to the world as a huge film set. The British capital hosted all the member nations of the International Olympic Committee, 204, for the first time in the history of the Games. It was also the first event in which all participants presented male and female delegations. 'This is a major boost for gender equality,' IOC President Jacques Rogge said, after Saudi Arabia, Qatar and Brunei confirmed the presence of women in their teams. For Rogge, it was about fulfilling 'a human right'. 'Opening the Olympic Games to more women is not just a matter of basic fairness. The Games provide a global platform for female Olympians that inspires others to follow their example. More than four billion people, well over half of the world's population, will have access to the London Games on television, the internet or their mobile devices. About half of that audience will be women and girls, a gender balance few other major sporting events can hope to match. That global reach makes the Games a powerful force for gender equality. Sport cannot cure all of society's ills. We do not have the power to bring gender equality to all aspects of human interaction. But we can use sport to help girls and young women gain the confidence to challenge stereotypes that limit their opportunities in other endeavours,' he said.

In London, 10,523 athletes fought for 302 gold medals corresponding to 26 sports: 5864 were men and 4659 women, almost 44.3 per cent of the participants. In addition, all sports included women's categories, counting boxing, a specialty that previously left no place for girls.

The medalist table was dominated, once again, by the United States, a country that conquered 104 medals (46 golds, 29 silvers and 29 bronzes). China with 87 medals (38 golds), host Britain with 65 medals (29 golds) and Russia with 82 medals (24 golds) were second, third and fourth, respectively. Of the 204 intervening nations, 84 returned home with at least one medal. In addition, a total of 32 new world records were registered in various sports such as swimming, athletics, weightlifting, shooting, archery, cycling and modern pentathlon.

The American swimmer Michael Phelps and the Jamaican sprinter Usain Bolt were crowned again as the top stars of the competition. Phelps accumulated 4 gold and 2 silver medals and, although he did not repeat the extraordinary 2008 harvest, he became the athlete with the highest number of medals in the history of the Games. The swimmer added a total of 22 medals between the Games of Athens 2004 and London 2012 (18 golds, 2 silvers and 2 bronzes) and with the 6 obtained in Great Britain he moved Ukrainian gymnast Larisa Latynina from the first place on the podium. Latynina had totaled 18 between the Melbourne 1956 and Tokyo 1964 editions. The remarkable production of Phelps is exacerbated when computing only the golden prizes, because he had doubled his closest follower's harvest in the general table: Latynina, the Finnish runner Paavo Nurmi and two other Americans, swimmer Mark Spitz and sprinter Carl Lewis, who 'barely' obtained 9.

Bolt, meanwhile, traced his excellent record of Beijing: 3 golds in the 100 meters, 200 meters and the 4x100 relay. With his invaluable contribution, Jamaica was the sensation of speed: gold and silver in

100-meter male (Yohan Blake was second); complete podium in 200 meters (Bolt, Blake and Warren Weir, respectively); gold in the 4x100 relay (Bolt, Blake, Nesta Carter and Michael Frater); gold and bronze in the female 100 meters (Shelly–Ann, Fraser–Pryce and Veronica Campbell–Brown), silver in the 200 meters (Fraser–Pryce) and in the 4x100 relay.

THE OLD COOKIE

At sixty-five years of age, Canadian Ian Millar achieved a unique record: he participated in ten Olympic Games. Millar, who always competed in equestrian jumps, began his extensive career in Munich 1972. Since then, he was always 'present' until London 2012, except in Moscow 1980, because his country joined the US-led boycott against the Soviet regime. In the British capital, Millar left behind two athletes who also added nine Games, although they had already retired: the Austrian sailor Hubert Raudaschl and the Latvian shooter Afanasijs Kuzmins, who represented the former Soviet Union in three of the competitions. Unfortunately for the Canadian, his performance was not that virtuous: he barely achieved a silver medal (Beijing 2008) in the team event. In London, Millar finished ninth in the individual competition and fifth in the team tournament.

WHEN ALL TRIED TO LOSE

The judges and supervisors of the women's double badminton tournament noted that there was something uncanny about the three games played on 31 July at the Wembley Arena. First, it was Indonesian Greysia Polii and Meiliana Jauhari and the South Koreans Kim Min-jun and Ha Jungeun, two couples already qualified for the quarter-finals, who were defeated by weaker rivals. Then, it got repeated in the duel between the Chinese Yu Yang and Wang Xiaoli and the South Korean

Hung Kyung-eun and Kim Ha-na, two couples already qualified for the next secured round, made rookie's mistakes. Their performances were so poor that the audience booed the participants and one of the judges stopped the first set of the match to demand that they compete seriously. 'They played to lose,' the referees then agreed after analysing the behaviours of the four couples. As a result of a report raised by the supervisors, the Badminton World Federation quickly studied the situation and concluded that, in effect, the four couples had tried to be defeated to avoid crossings with stronger rivals in the following round, a direct elimination stage from the quarter-finals. The girls were accused of 'not putting all their effort to win the game' and 'behaving in a clearly abusive manner to the detriment of the sport'.

'There is no place in the Olympic Games for a behaviour like this,' IOC spokesman Mark Adams said categorically. The eight players who wanted to lose were finally pleased: all were eliminated from the contest.

EVERYTHING ENDS IN THE ASHES

At the beginning of September 2006, the Australian national, George Gordon Avery, summoned his daughter to the bed where he lay very ill, and expressed his desire to return to London to relive the Olympic event that he had starred successfully in 1948. Back then, Avery had won the silver medal in triple jump after being behind the Swedish Arne Åhman, gold winner, for just 3.5 centimeters. The disease worsened and the former athlete died a few days later at the age of eighty-one. However, the dry death did not prevent Avery from being, in some way, at the great 2012 Olympic date. Robyn Glynn, his daughter, had the body creamed, and traveled to London with the ashes, her sister, their respective husbands and grandchildren of the former athlete to witness the triple jump contest that took place on 9 August at the Olympic Stadium. When the competition ended—with the victory of the American Christian Taylor—Robyn approached to the track, took the box with the remains of her father and spread the ashes through the sports field, just above the section destined for the triple jump tournament. 'We knew this was the place he wanted to return to. He wanted very much to be here,' the woman confided to ABC radio. Almost sixty-four years after being on the podium, Avery returned to London and stayed forever in the place where, he admitted, he achieved the greatest happiness of his life.

BLACK BELT SPECTATOR

On 5 August at the Olympic Stadium, a man named Ashley Gill-Webb was seated drunk among the spectators. Seconds before the start of the final of the 100-meter race, Gill-Webb got up from his seat and threw a bottle of beer, though empty and of plastic, to the Jamaican sprinter Usain Bolt. The athlete did not notice the audacity, but the Dutch, Edith Bosch did: she was sitting a few meters away from the troublemaker. Very determined, Bosch stood up, headed towards Gill-Webb and gave a blow to the head that knocked out the drunkard. Then, two policemen showed up at the scene and took the humiliated bully and arrested him. This story, narrated like this, seems a Disney tale. However, it is fair to say that Bosch was not a Pocahontas or a Snow White: four days before the incident, the Dutchwoman had won the bronze medal in judo, in the category of up to 70 kilos. In addition to the punch, Gill-Webb received an eight-week sentence of community work and was forced to pay a fine of 1500 British pounds.

ON ONE LEG

The US athletic team started the 4x400 relay with the left foot, almost literally: Manteo Mitchell, the runner of the initial lap, fractured the left leg fibula while participating in the first qualifying race. About halfway, the athlete stomped and the bone exploded. 'I felt like someone had broken my leg,' Mitchell told to the reporters at the end of the qualifying tests. But, despite the tremendous injury, Mitchell did not resign and continued running the 200 meters that separated him from the companion who was waiting for the baton, the metal bar that must be passed to the next runner in this kind of race. Even with such a disadvantage, the American quartet qualified in the first place of the series. 'Three guys depended on me, I couldn't let them down!' said the injured sprinter. Thanks to Mitchell's tremendous effort, the United States reached the final, where Bryshon Nellum, Joshua Mance, Tony McQuay and his replacement, Angelo Taylor, won the silver medal.

PRINCE AND PAUPER

Few Olympic champions have lived a celebration as poorly as the German Robert Harting, winner of gold medal in discus throw. On the afternoon of 7 August, after beating the Iranian Ehsan Haddadi by 9 centimeters in the final round, Harting was the center of a series of entertainment that included a toast at the 'Deutsches Haus' (German House), the fan fest and headquarters of the German delegation mounted on the banks of the Thames. While the champion signed autographs and posed for the fans with his medal around his neck, a light-fingered got into his sports bag and seized the official identification of the athlete. After the tribute, the discobolus returned alone to the Olympic Village to rest in his room, but at the door of the place discovered that someone had taken the accreditation that allowed him to pass through the entrance. To make matters worse, the rigid guards of the villa were not convinced of the passport, the Harting explanations and even the gold medal attesting to the Olympic title. The agents were ordered not to let anyone pass without a credential, and they complied strictly with the regulation. Moreover, at that time, the accreditation office was closed, so the German athlete had to wait until 8 am in the morning to process a new credential. Evicted and exhausted, Harting went to a subway station next to the Olympic Village and spent the night sleeping on the bench of one of the platforms! 'I have been robbed when I was with the fans,' he denounced through his Twitter account before closing his eyes and enjoying his 'champion's dream' on a hard mattress.

DUMB MEDALIST

Felipe Kitadai was exultant with his bronze medal. The Brazilian judoca walked back and forth with his prize hanging around his neck for everyone to congratulate him. He boasted through Hall 2 of the ExCeL Exhibition Center, the Olympic Village and even inside his room, when he got into the shower without clothes and only with the medal around his neck. Before opening the faucet, Kitadai tried to take off his medal to prevent it from getting wet, but with such awkwardness that the ribbon was hooked, it ripped and the prize flew out and fell against the floor ceramics, where it broke in half. Disconsolate by the 'accident', the judoca asked the Olympic Committee of his country to intercede before the IOC to ask for a new medal. 'I feel like the child whose new toy is broken,' he confessed miserably. The IOC analysed the case, and after taking pity on the clumsy judoca, decided to award a new medal to the negligent Brazilian athlete, but not before warning him to be more careful.

RIO DE JANEIRO 2016

The first South American Games will be remembered for the goodbye of two sports Olympian gods: Jamaican sprinter Usain Bolt and American swimmer Michael Phelps. The Caribbean runner picked three more golds for his extraordinary career, but then lost one, the one corresponding to the 4x100 relay, because one of his teammates, Nesta Carter, tested positive in the doping test. Bolt, who would later leave the tracks to continue as a professional footballer in a Norwegian club, left the athletics with a hard-to-beat track record: eight gold medals in three Olympic editions. Phelps, meanwhile, won five competitions and raised his magnificent golden production to twenty-three. In the Brazilian Games, the 'Baltimore Shark' also collected a silver medal, which helped round a total of twenty-eight medals.

The competition suffered, however, some setbacks. Like the 2014 World Cup in Brazil, the event encountered local and international corruption reports. Numerous newspaper articles disseminated investigations that revealed alleged deviations of funds for infrastructure works to private pockets. The President of the Brazilian Olympic Committee, Carlos Arthur Nuzman, was also accused of paying bribes to leaders of other countries so that Rio de Janeiro won the election over other cities nominated for the big sporting event, such as Chicago or Madrid.

Days before the start of the competitions, the International Athletics Federation rejected the requests of sixty-seven Russian competitors, suspected of having used prohibited substances to improve their performance. In addition, rowers, pentathletes, weightlifters, fighters and even a sailor were excluded, all sanctioned by their respective sports associations. The scandal which involved more than a hundred athletes broke out when Grigory Rodchenkov, former head of the Moscow anti-doping laboratory, fled to the United States and denounced an institutional doping program that, according to his accusation, was supervised by the Kremlin. Rodchenkov—incorporated into an FBI witness protection program, because he was afraid of being killed—said that Russian President Vladimir Putin was aware of the practices that, according to his testimony, were carried out in his country since the 2008 Beijing Olympics.

Let us return, better, to the very essence of the competition, because Rio de Janeiro was also the scene of wide smiles. Throughout the competition, sixty-five Olympic records and nineteen world marks were broken. In addition to the huge collection of Phelps, which created a record that seems eternal, the American Katie Ledecky set two world records in the pool, in the 400-meter medley (3:58.57) and in the 800-meter medley (8:04.79). In weightlifting, two successes traveled to China, thanks to Qingquan Long in the male category of 56 kilos and Wei Deng in the female of 63 kilos.

Meanwhile, the American shooter Kimberly Rhode recorded her name in Olympic history as the first woman to win medal in six consecutive Olympics. Rhode won the gold in the double trap event in Atlanta 1996—making her the youngest female gold medalist in the history of Olympic shooting—and in Athens 2004, and was champion also in London 2012 but in the skeet contest. She also obtained a silver in Sydney 2000 (double trap) and in Beijing

2008 (skeet). In Rio de Janeiro, the American won the bronze in skeet.

The greatest joy of the local fans exploded in the magnificent Maracana Stadium, where the football team won the only prize lacked in its glass cabinet: the Olympic gold medal. The achievement was resolved through a penalty shoot-out, since the final game, against Germany, ended up tied in a goal after two hours of play. Brazil took revenge of a defeat suffered two years earlier in the World Cup semi final: in Belo Horizonte, the German squad had imposed a humiliating score of 7–1 on the host team.

KNOCKED DOWN BY HIS OWN MARE

When Ian Millar approached to his eleventh Olympic game at the age of sixty-nine, his mare Dickson left him on foot. The 'Captain Canada', winner of a silver medal in the category of team equestrian jumps in Beijing 2008, began his Olympic career at the age of twenty-five in the 1972 Munich Games, and was only absent in Moscow 1980, because of the boycott promoted by the USA, adhered by his country. Although he had qualified for the great Rio event, Millar had to abdicate because Dickson became ill and had to be operated, and did not have an animal prepared to compete at the highest level. The rider traveled to Rio de Janeiro anyway, as coach of the Canadian team. His position was taken by his daughter Amy, who starred in a rather weak performance: mounted on her horse Heros, the girl competed in the individual jumping contest without qualifying for the final round. Amy's poor performance also affected the team, which stayed off the podium, in the fourth place.

CURIOUS ACCIDENT

Hiroki Ogita, in a pink uniform and blue sneakers, raised his pole to perform his last jump in the qualifying phase of Group A of the pole vault tournament. The Japanese athlete, who had already failed in all his previous attempts, began his career, gained speed and made a magnificent jump: his legs exceeded the bar located 5.45 meters from the ground. However, at the start of the descent, one of his thighs brushed the rod, which barely trembled. Nothing serious. The real problem arose a few thousandths of a second later, when the ribbon fell driven by a portion of the Asian jumper's member. The unusual incident not only cost Ogita his elimination of the competition, but it went viral on social networks. The japanese competitor, who finished in twenty-first place, knocked down the rod…with his penis!

HALF BAREFOOT

The Barein runner Ruth Jebet won the gold medal in the women's 3000-meter steeplechase race. The Kenyan Hyvin Jepkemoi was left with the silver, the American Emma Coburn with the bronze and the Ethiopian Etenesh Diro, with the highest ovation from the Carioca public. Why? In the middle of the athletic competition, held on 15 August at the Nilton Santos Olympic Stadium, the good Diro lost a shoe. The incident happened while the African runner occupied the vanguard squad: there was a clash between several participants and Diro not only fell to the track, but also her right footwear disappeared between legs and bodies. Far from being intimidated, the girl rejoined and continued the race with a singular march—one foot naked, the other covered by a shoe- until she reached the finishing line in position 15, almost 40 seconds after the winner. Diro did not take a medal or diploma but the recognition of the spectators in applause.

BEAT THE IDOL

When a photo was taken with US multi-champion Michael Phelps in 2008, Singaporean teenager Joseph Schooling did not imagine what the future would hold to him. Encouraged by his hero, the Asian kid adopted a passion for swimming and prepared for several years to fulfil his dream: to be an Olympic athlete. The boy felt hard and in 2016 he received the great opportunity to make his wishes come true: Schooling, twenty-one, qualified to represent his homeland in the great competition that would take place at the Olympic Aquatic Stadium in Rio de Janeiro. In the 100-meter butterfly contest, the Singaporean swimmer passed the first round with ease. Then, he won the semi-final 2, with a time of 50.83 seconds. In the final, Schooling had to swim along the lane number 4. Along number 2 was his idol. The shot rang and the Asian swimmer fixed a time that was an Olympic record: 50.39. The student surpassed the teacher by thirty-five hundredths of a second; the silver medal was held by Michael Phelps.

FATAL CELEBRATION

Sinphet Kruaithong was pure joy. The 56-kg Thai weightlifter had just won a bronze medal—the first one won by a male weightlifter from his country in the Olympic history—and he knew that in his native rural village, in the Chumphon Buri district, everyone would celebrate his conquest. What the boy could not imagine was that, in his homeland, that day there was no happiness: his grandmother Subin, who had met with other relatives and neighbours to watch Sinphet's performance on television, died of a heart attack when she saw her grandson climbing on the podium. The eighty-four-year-old woman's heart could not controlso much emotion.

RESCUED BY HANDBALL PLAYERS

Argentine tennis player Juan Martín del Potro took the elevator of his building in the Olympic Village to go to the tennis court where he had to face the number 1 of the male ranking and favourite to win the tournament, Novak Djokovic, for the first round of the individual championship. In the middle of the descent, the device ran out of energy and stopped between two floors. Trapped in the dark, with no signal on his mobile phone, Del Potro appealed to the only resource he had to escape from the incident: scream. His yelps, fortunately, were heard by some of their compatriots, members of the Olympic handball team. The athletes managed to unlock the doors and rescue the tennis player after about forty minutes. The strange event did not affect Del Potro, who shortly after defeated Djokovic in two sets. The adventure, even, seemed to have revitalised the Argentine, who continued his winning road until the final, in which he had to settle for the silver medal after falling to the Scott, Andy Murray.

ACKNOWLEDGEMENTS

My sincere thanks goes to José Luis Cutello for his precise advices. I am grateful to Ignacio Iraola for supporting and promoting this project. Also thanks to Eduardo Galeano for always being there. And to Nadia, for everything.

BIBLIOGRAPHY

- Cousineau, Phil; *Olympic Odyssey*. Quest Books, Wheaton Illinois, 2003.
- Goldblatt, David; *The Ball is Round*. Penguin Books, London, 2006.
- Guttmann, Allen; *The Olympics*. University of Illinois Press, Champaign, 2002.
- Hill, Christopher; *Olympic Politics*. Manchester University Press, Manchester, 1992.
- Maraniss, David; *Rome 1960, The Summer Olympics That Stirred the World*. Simon & Schuster Paperbacks, New York, 2008.
- Martin, David, y Gynn, Roger; *The Olympic Marathon*. Human Kinetics, Champaign, 2000.
- Payne, Michael; *Olympic Turnaround*. Praeger Publishers, Westport, 2006.
- Perrottet, Tony; *The Naked Olympics*. Random House, New York, 2004.
- Risolo, Donn; *Soccer Stories*. Board of Regents of the University of Nebraska, Lincoln, 2010.
- Sirracos, Constantine; *History of the Olympic Games*. Seaburn Publishing Group, New York, 2002.
- Swaddling, Judith; *The Ancient Olympic Games*. University of Texas Press, Austin, 2008.
- Tibballs, Geoff; *The Olympics' Strangest Moments*. Robson Books, London, 2004.
- Wernicke, Luciano; *Historias insólitas de los Mundiales de fútbol*. Editorial Planeta, Buenos Aires, 2010.

NEWSPAPERS

- Argentina: *Clarín, La Nación, Olé, Diario Popular, Crónica, La Prensa, La Razón, Uno.*
- Australia: *Weekly Times*
- Canada: *Toronto Star, The Expositor.*
- France: *L'Équipe.*
- Spain: *As, Marca, El Mundo, El País, La Vanguardia, El Mundo Deportivo.*
- United States of America: *New York Times, New York Post, Los Ángeles Times, Los Ángeles Sentinel.*
- Mexico: *La Crónica de Hoy.*
- Norway: *Verdens Gang.*
- Puerto Rico: *Primera Hora.*
- United Kingdom: *Daily Mail, The Times, Evening Stardard, Daily Telegraph, Daily Mirror, The Independent.*
- Southafrica: *Mail & Guardian.*

MAGAZINES

- *El Gráfico* (Argentina)
- *Campeón* (Argentina)
- *Mundo deportivo* (Argentina)
- *Selecciones* (Argentina)
- *Life* (United States of America)
- *Sports Illustrated* (United States of America)
- *Newsweek* (United States of America)
- *Jet* (United States of America)
- *Black Belt* (United States of America)

NEWS AGENCIES

- Diarios y Noticias (DyN-Argentina)
- Reuters (United Kingdom)
- Deutsche Presse Agentur (DPA-Germany)
- EFE (Spain)
- Agence France Press (AFP-France)
- Agenzia Nazionale Stampa Associata (ANSA-Italia)
- United Press International (UPI- United States of America)
- Asociated Press (AP, United States of America).